ERING
'ER'S WAY

Comfort those who grieve:

Ministering God's grace
in times of loss

Paul Tautges

DayOne

©Day One Publications 2009
First printed 2009
Reprinted 2012

Scripture quotations taken from the New American Standard Bible®, Copyright © 1960, 1962, 1963, 1968, 1971, 1972, 1973, 1975, 1977, 1995 by The Lockman Foundation. Used by permission. (www.Lockman.org)

A CIP record is held at the British Library

ISBN 978-1-84625-155-9

Published by Day One Publications, Ryelands Road, Leominster, HR6 8NZ
☎ 01568 613 740
FAX 01568 611 473
email—sales@dayone.co.uk
web site—www.dayone.co.uk
North American e-mail—usasales@dayone.co.uk
North American web site—www.dayonebookstore.com

Cover designed by Wayne McMaster
Printed by Orchard Press Cheltenham Ltd

ENDORSEMENTS

Pastor Paul Tautges is a man with a mission—a mission to minister to the broken-hearted. He's as comfortable carrying out this mission on a large scale (funerals and memorial services) as he is on an individual, personal scale. In both cases, he is careful to offer a blend of sensitive concern with a proclamation of the gospel in clear, honest language. His thoughts on the theology of grief, the sermons and the practical charts included in this book may prove helpful to those pastors who search for ways to improve this part of their own ministries. This book gives us a glimpse into the heart of a pastor who possesses a love for his flock, a sound grasp of the Scriptures and a calling to comfort the hurting in a biblical, compassionate way.

> **Deborah Howard, RN, Certified Hospice and Palliative Nurse, and author of** Sunsets: Reflections for Life's Final Journey, It's Not Fair! *(co-authored by Dr. Wayne Mack) and* Where Is God in All of This?

Few have attempted to offer comfort to those who grieve, and fewer have been as successful as Pastor Paul Tautges in this much-needed book. I commend this wonderful little volume. It is a veritable anthology of practical helps for those who are grieving and for those who attempt to minister to their needs. Therefore I recommend it as a book for all deacons, elders, pastors and lay persons. It is an important tool which should be thoughtfully read if we are to minister wisely and effectively to those in our fellowship who will eventually face such times.

> **Dr. Walter C. Kaiser, Jr., President Emeritus, Gordon-Conwell Theological Seminary, Hamilton, Massachusetts, USA**

Paul Tautges, in his book Comfort Those Who Grieve, *gives pastors and other compassionate caregivers a very unusual and much-needed book—one that is thoroughly biblical and immensely practical. He teaches us how to biblically comfort hurting and dying people. Every minister of the gospel will find it helpful. Pastor Tautges offers us specific ways in which we can carry out this task, including pertinent Scriptures, hymns, and poems to use. He has even prepared an extended follow-up plan for ministering to those left behind following the death of a loved one. We are given concrete ideas for consoling those who are dying and on preparing funeral messages which not only comfort the grieving, but also challenge the lost with a clear gospel message. I know of no book like* Comfort Those Who Grieve. *Most "how to" books are shallow and often devoid of deep theological content. This excellent book is an exception. After over fifty years in the ministry, I learned much from Pastor Tautges and wish that I could have read it much earlier.*

> **Curtis C. Thomas, *pastor for over fifty years, Bible teacher, and author of* Life in the Body**

Here is biblical, insightful, and practical advice regarding serving those who grieve. Written with the tenderness and understanding of a gentle pastor, this book will be a helpful manual for those who guide others through the valley of the shadow of death. I hope it gains wide distribution!

> **Dr. Les Lofquist, IFCA International Executive Director**

Dedication
To the memory of Jean Pitz,
a dear sister in the Lord,
who always had a word of encouragement
for this preacher of the gospel
and who would never exchange her place in
Glory for anything this world has to offer
&
to hospice caregivers everywhere,
who sacrificially give of themselves from the heart
in order to help others comfortably live
through the experience of death.

A WORD OF THANKS

I thank the patient flock that God has called me to shepherd, Immanuel Bible Church in Sheboygan, Wisconsin for allowing me to show my frail humanity by grieving with them in times of earthly loss. I am especially grateful to Jerome Pitz, for being supportive of my desire to dedicate this book to the memory of his wife, Jean, and to include certain parts of her memorial service; to Jackie Arnoldi, for permitting me to share the poem she wrote in honor of her mother; to William and Carolyn Freel, for their willingness to let me include the Bible meditation given at their newborn son's memorial service; to Ken Dolezal, for permitting me to include a personal letter to a grieving brother; and to Jonathan Allston, for the lyrics to his song, "O Refuge Near," a fitting theme for this book. When "one member suffers, all the members suffer with it; if one member is honored, all the members rejoice with it" (1 Cor. 12:26).

I also thank other servants in my church for their assistance with this book: Linda Baalke, Eric Liederbach, Sandy Saberniak, and Ashley Tautges. "For even the Son of Man did not come to be served, but to serve" (Mark 10:45).

I again thank Jim Holmes of Day One Publications for his enthusiasm for the Ministering the Master's Way series and for requesting this manuscript earlier than I expected, which was used by the Holy Spirit to deepen my own walk of faith. I also thank Mrs. Suzanne Mitchell for her assistance as my editor. Both of these servants have encouraged me immensely. "As each one has received a special gift, employ it in serving one another as good stewards of the manifold grace of God" (1 Peter 4:10).

I thank hospice nurse and author Deborah Howard for her helpful comments and suggestions. Since she ministers to the dying on a daily basis and has written on the subject of grief ministry, her input has been invaluable. "Therefore encourage one another and build up one another, just as you also are doing" (1 Thes. 5:11).

CONTENTS

A PERSONAL TESTIMONY

Death is a very real and natural part of life. We all die, and there is no stopping it. Our loved ones die, and there is no escaping the grief we experience and the pain that lingers in our hearts because we miss them so much. How do we get through such difficult times? I would like to share with you my family's story and how we have dealt, and still are dealing, with our loss.

On Saturday, April 12, 2008 my family and I suffered a very difficult loss. My wonderful mother, Jean Pitz, died of cancer at only fifty-four years of age. She was diagnosed only ten months earlier. When they found it, the cancer had already spread and was considered very aggressive. She barely made it through the initial diagnosis in the hospital and we nearly lost her several times before God miraculously brought her through in response to the prayers of His people.

The months afterward were very difficult, as we knew that her time with us was short (probably less than a year). God was so gracious to give us very special times with my mother before she died—time to hug, hold hands, and say "I love you" just one more time. Yet sometimes we lose loved ones more tragically and without warning. Just six years earlier, my dear cousin, Rachel, died in a terrible car accident when she was only twenty-four years old. This left all who loved her devastated and in complete shock. There were no last chances or last words—death just intruded into our family.

Many of you reading this book can relate to one of these situations or at least know of someone who has gone through something similar. These stories abound. Many people are hurting because of the death of a loved one. Sometimes God allows our lives to get flipped upside down and we don't always know why. Did God leave His throne when these things were happening? No. Did He make a mistake? No. Is He unloving or cruel to let such things happen to us? Absolutely not! He is very much in control. We may not see His purpose for what we are going through, and we may not ever see all the reasons why He does what He does. He is God and our minds cannot fully comprehend His ways: "Oh, the depth of the riches both of the wisdom and knowledge of God! How unsearchable are His judgments and unfathomable His ways!" (Rom. 11:33).

Knowing Jesus Christ as my personal Savior and the Lord of my life, I was able to cling to Him through these tough times. The Holy Spirit kept bringing to my mind the fact that God is sovereign and in control of every moment. I just needed to "cease striving and know that [He is] God" (Ps. 46:10) and to trust that He truly does cause "all things to work together for good to those who love God, to those who are called according to His purpose" (Rom. 8:28). As I continue to keep Christ as my focus through this trial, instead of focusing on myself and my pain, I will see God's goodness and some of His purposes for it. I need to believe that through the trial He is refining me, making me more like His Son. I'm not saying that I don't ever fall apart. I certainly have hard days, and the pain can be numbing because I miss my mother so much. But I also have hope when I reflect on such verses as Psalm 94:19: "When my anxious thoughts multiply within me, Your consolations delight my soul."

God's Word: what a blessing in trial! Being in His Word is so crucial to our walk of faith. Not just *when* hardships come, but *before*, to prepare us for these times. The very Truth that it is gives us strength for each day. Sometimes verses impact us differently in our time of need than they have done before. We must not minimize how powerful His Word is to strengthen us in the storms of life.

One of the greatest blessings of going through the loss of my mother has been the overwhelming love of our church family at Immanuel Bible Church in Sheboygan, Wisconsin. Nothing can replace these precious brothers and sisters in Christ. They have bathed us in prayer. Not just once a day, but they have prayed "without ceasing" (1 Thes. 5:17). At one point, they held a forty-eight-hour prayer vigil for my mother in her most crucial moments. Someone was praying for her forty-eight hours straight! The pastor also called on the church to fast and pray on many occasions. It was so amazing to see the Lord working in our church body and the excitement that everyone had when my mother started to get better and was able to return to church for a short time. God is so good, and our church family has learned so much about boldly approaching the throne of God and crying out to Him earnestly. Psalm 61:1–2 says, "Hear my cry, O God; Give heed to my prayer. From the end of the earth I call to You when my heart is faint; Lead me to the rock that is higher than I." We also continue to learn of the necessity of true surrender to God in prayer as we repeat the words of Jesus: "not My will, but Yours be done" (Luke 22:42).

Not only do we have a very loving church family, but we also have a wonderful shepherd, Paul Tautges, whose wise leadership and close attention to our needs during this time have been a constant encouragement. A very caring church body is the product of a very caring pastor and friend. Never once have we felt overlooked or questioned whether he cares. He loves us with the love of Christ. He often goes for lunch with my father and sends cards, books, and other helpful information to our family on a regular basis.

It can be very difficult adjusting to the loss of a loved one, but God's grace is sufficient. As those redeemed by the blood of Christ, we need to be witnesses to the world around us. We need to show them God's goodness and faithfulness despite all the turmoil that surrounds us. How can we lead others to Christ if all they see is a life falling apart because there is no firm foundation? We have been created by God for God. Every circumstance is an opportunity to glorify Him—even the death of someone we love so dearly. "Blessed be the God and Father of our Lord Jesus Christ, the Father of mercies and God of all comfort, who comforts us in all our affliction so that we will be able to comfort those who are in any affliction with the comfort with which we ourselves are comforted by God" (2 Cor. 1:3–4).

Jackie Arnoldi

PREFACE

The writing of a book on the subject of comforting those who grieve was something I anticipated—for quite some time. Almost two decades of pastoral ministry and several years of service as a hospice chaplain have perhaps resulted in my having had more than average exposure to grief and death. So, I imagined that someday I might write on this topic. However, although I may have been mentally prepared to consider one day penning some words of encouragement to fellow ministers of grace, I was unprepared for it at this particular time. There is no way I could ever have predicted the specific circumstances that propelled this book into existence. Neither was I ready for the varied emotions that would accompany this project.

This book is dedicated to the memory of a sister in the Lord who was a vital part of our church family but who beat the rest of us to the finish line on April 12, 2008. After a courageous fight with cancer, she finished the race of faith earlier than anyone ever expected. We are confident, however, that she is now busy casting crowns at her Savior's feet as, together with believers of previous ages, she worships the Lamb of God. For this reason, this book is an unexpected labor of love—an important part of my own involvement in what is commonly referred to as "the grieving process." Paul Tripp is correct when he writes in his helpful booklet *Grief: Finding Hope Again*, "Death is an emotionally volatile event that is painful in unexpected ways. Death digs up buried memories. It brings some people together and drives others apart. It begins some things and ends others. Death mixes happiness with sadness."[1] Death provides a natural opportunity not only for ministry to others, but also for personal growth in ministers of the gospel as we ourselves experience the grief of a shepherd who has lost one of his sheep.

Hospice caregivers are also included in my dedication because of their exemplary compassion. God in His providence first exposed me to hospices during the first few years of my pastoral ministry. I don't remember how He opened the door for me to serve as a volunteer chaplain: it just happened, and to this day I'm glad it did. Through my exposure to hospices I have witnessed a side of the dying process that I had not seen before and, consequently, I have grown to appreciate those who give themselves to this invaluable service.

Until the end of time, when the curse of sin will be finally removed, suffering will be a large part of the human experience. It is essential, therefore, that every believer be equipped to serve others with the grace of Christ. We are all "comforters-in-training." If this book encourages your personal growth as a minister of God's grace, then my joy will be complete. Together, may we continue to "grow in the grace and knowledge of our Lord and Savior Jesus Christ" (2 Peter 3:18), to whom belongs all glory and honor.

Introduction

Why should I feel discouraged, why should the
  shadows come,
Why should my heart be lonely, and long for
  heav'n and home,
When Jesus is my portion? My constant Friend is He:
His eye is on the sparrow, and I know He watches me.

–Cevilla D. Martin[1]

The morning I sat down to begin working on the final version of this book, my friend's father had begun his last day. Within a couple of hours, he was in the presence of Jesus. Death is painfully real. It is not foreign territory upon which ministers of grace walk. We would have to be cold, callous, or uninvolved in people's lives not to be affected by death. And we would lack compassion if we did not possess a desire to reach out with the Christ-centered comfort of God to those who grieve. This priority has been freshly implanted in my mind in the year of writing this book, as God has brought the members of my congregation face to face with death on numerous occasions.

What many refer to as the gospel portion of the book of Isaiah begins with these words: "'Comfort, O comfort My people,' says your God" (Isa. 40:1). Isaiah has earned the nickname "the evangelical prophet" because of his emphasis on the good news of the coming Messiah—the hope and strong comfort of Israel. With reference to this verse, Warren Wiersbe explains, "The English word 'comfort' comes from two Latin words that together mean 'with strength.' When Isaiah says to us, 'Be comforted!' it is not a word of pity but of power. God's comfort does not weaken us; it strengthens us. God is not indulging us but empowering us."[2]

Overwhelmed by their failure, and by the sin which brought

about severe chastisement, the people of God were in desperate need of hope—the hope of God's pardon. Verse 2 continues,

> Speak kindly to Jerusalem;
> And call out to her, that her warfare has ended,
> That her iniquity has been removed,
> That she has received of the LORD's hand
> Double for all her sins.

The hope that Isaiah gives is rooted in God's relationship to Israel as His people: "'Comfort *My* people,' says *your* God." Though His people's sin was indeed worthy of a double portion of divine discipline, God was not about to turn His back on them. He would fulfill the covenant that He had made. Later, through the mouth of Jeremiah, God again dispenses hope in the midst of Israel's pain: "'For I know the plans that I have for you,' declares the Lord, 'plans for welfare and not for calamity to give you a future and a hope'" (Jer. 29:11). By turning their focus away from their past, as well as from their present, toward the future hope of the promised kingdom, both prophets provided Messiah-centered comfort.

Since we live *after* the cross of Calvary, we might call it "Christ-centered comfort." But the principle is very much the same. The strength of God's comfort does not come from His ability to change our present circumstances (which He can do if He chooses), but rather from the promise that He has made to us in Christ: He will finish the transformational work that He started in us, and the glory that we will one day share with Him far outweighs our present suffering (Phil. 1:6; Rom. 8:18). In other words, gospel-centered comfort is the only true comfort there is. Any comfort we give to people outside the hope of the gospel is temporary at best and deceptive at worst. If we merely dispense earthly comfort to those who are suffering and fall short of pointing them to the only true source of comfort, Jesus Christ, we have potentially deceived them into thinking that God is on their side when in fact He may not be. If they are unbelievers, then they are still God's enemies, and we have offered them no lasting comfort at all unless we have pointed them to the "man of sorrows" who is "acquainted with grief" (Isa. 53:3).

This gospel-centered hope faces the reality of death head-on by holding forth the gift of eternal life that Jesus purchased with His own blood. If we fail to gently speak the truth of the gospel at a time like this, we have not made death our servant as we ought. Instead, we must correctly seize each divinely ordained ministry opportunity by utilizing earthly pain to redirect the bereaved to focus on eternal matters. Joni Eareckson Tada and Steve Estes write in their book *When God Weeps*, "Earth's pain keeps crushing our hopes, reminding us this world can never satisfy; only heaven can. And every time we begin to nestle too comfortably on this planet, God cracks open the locks of the dam to allow an ice-cold splash of suffering to wake us from our spiritual slumber."[3] Let us not waste these precious and painful occasions that are given to us for the demonstration of mercy and the advantage of the gospel.

Part 1: Sovereign God of comfort

Every minister of God's grace must be committed to establishing a doctrinal foundation for his people that will provide them with an anchor to grip during the storms of life. They also need the deep theological roots that grow by means of regular preaching on the absolute sovereignty of God over every event in our lives, along with teaching on the personal care that God has for His children—from the day of our birth to the day of our death.

The following four chapters are samples of ways to minister God's grace, not only at the actual time of a person's greatest need, but also beforehand, so that this sure foundation is laid for that person's faith. Hospice caregiver Deborah Howard RN, CHPN has written a precious book entitled *Sunsets: Reflections on Life's Final Journey*, in which she writes, "We must have the essential faith and trust in God *before* our hearts are broken. Then we will possess the tools needed to understand and deal with the situation *without being devastated*."[1] As faithful and loving ministers, we must prepare God's people to face life's dangers with a vigorous faith in the sovereign God of comfort.

These examples of sermons are included at the start of this book in order to establish the conviction that if we are going to be ministers of God's grace in times of loss, we must be both truth-filled witnesses and loving shepherds. We must be faithful to speak forth the Word of God so that our fellow Christians have a rock-solid foundation upon which to build their lives. But we must also be sensitive shepherds who walk our sheep through the dark valley of suffering, especially the darkest one—death itself—with the comfort of God. As we serve them with compassion, God will use us to instill a biblical hope and confidence that matches that of the psalmist:

> Even though I walk through the valley of the
> shadow of death,

I fear no evil, for You are with me;
Your rod and Your staff, they comfort me.

Ps. 23:4

Chapter 1 gives an exposition of Psalm 46 and serves as an example of the kinds of messages that we as ministers need to regularly feed our people. While maintaining the practice of preaching verse by verse through books of the Bible (the best way to provide a steady diet of the Word of God to believers), we must also be flexible enough to drop back from our sermon series momentarily in order to act upon pastoral awareness so that the pressing needs within our flocks are addressed biblically. We must provide healthy doses of pastoral care through sensitive preaching. Nothing accomplishes this more effectively than preaching on the twofold reality of God's absolute sovereignty *and* His tender care for those whom He has redeemed to be His own. Because many of the songs the Holy Spirit preserved for us in the book of Psalms were birthed out of human pain and tragedy, this balance abounds in that portion of God's Word and, therefore, it should be turned to often.

Chapter 2 gives an example of preaching that is based on a hymn. This occasional approach to our teaching ministry weds rich theology (health-giving doctrine) to pastoral tenderness. In this case, the stanzas of the hymn "Be Still, My Soul" become the main points in the sermon, which are used to direct the minds of the listeners to certain biblical truths which the preacher then expounds. Other great hymns of the faith that might serve this purpose well include "Great Is Thy Faithfulness" (Thomas O. Chisholm), "It Is Well with My Soul" (Horatio G. Spafford), "I Am His and He Is Mine" (Wade Robinson), "Day By Day" (Karolina Sandell-Berg; tr. Andrew L. Skoog), "God Leads us Along" (G. A. Young) and others that speak of God's protective care for His children.

Chapter 3 shows an example of what could be preached to a

congregation when it first hears of the death of a church member. "God's Delight in the Death of a Believer" is a compilation of several condensed expositions that provide immediate comfort to those who grieve. Though I do not make the writing of prayers a normal practice, the closing prayers from these sermon transcripts are included here because we must not underestimate the importance of biblically informed prayer *with* those in need. This kind of intercessory prayer is an essential part of a biblical ministry of comfort. Walter Kaiser is convinced that "when all is said and done we rest our case for relief and healing from suffering when we commit it to God in prayer."[2] Consequently, those who grieve need us to carry them to God's throne of grace at all times, but especially when they may be too frail or fearful to take themselves there. Prayer is indispensable to both public ministry, in the corporate gatherings of the church family, and to private ministry, at the bedsides of dying members.

Chapter 4 is a pastoral letter written to a man in my congregation who lost both his parents and suffered a stroke all within six months. It is an example of the kind of personal care that believers need from their ministers at certain places on their walk with God.

A refuge in the time of storm

Chapter 1

O refuge near, our strength in weakness, forever in
   His hands secure;
Emmanuel, God always with us, Almighty One
   within my soul.
I'll never fear the roaring waters; the tempests
   know the One in me.
The hands that hold the stars in motion are
   holding me in love and care.

–Jonathan Allston[I]

The hymn-writer hit the nail on the head when he wrote, "How firm a foundation, ye saints of the Lord, is laid for your faith in His excellent Word!"[2] His words were undoubtedly influenced by those of the apostle Peter, who assures us that "we have the prophetic word made more sure" than the most dramatic spiritual experience (2 Peter 1:19). There is no time in our lives as believers when this secure base of biblical truth is more necessary than when we or someone we love stands at the door of death. Therefore, as God's ministers, we are most faithful when we diligently teach the Word of God. The following exposition of Psalm 46, and its application to the ministry of comfort, serves as an example of how the Scriptures build this reliable foundation for the believer's faith.

Where do you run to when the storms of life beat upon you with unrelenting persistence? Where do you hide when trouble chases you like a hound pursuing a fox? Where do you find peace when fear overtakes you and anxiety places its tight grip around your neck? Where do you go when grief casts its dark shadow over your faith? The answer to all four questions is the same—or, at least, it should be. It is *God*. We must run to God. We must hide in God. We must find peace and rest *in God* while our souls wrestle and hurt inside. He alone is the One who can meet our deepest needs while He nurtures us and teaches us what it really means to trust Him with every trial. As the psalmist writes:

> ¹God is our refuge and strength,
>   A very present help in trouble.
> ²Therefore we will not fear, though the earth should change
>   And though the mountains slip into the heart of the sea;
> ³Though its waters roar and foam,
>   Though the mountains quake at its swelling pride. Selah.
> ⁴There is a river whose streams make glad the city of God,
>   The holy dwelling places of the Most High.
> ⁵God is in the midst of her, she will not be moved;
>   God will help her when morning dawns.
> ⁶The nations made an uproar, the kingdoms tottered;
>   He raised His voice, the earth melted.
> ⁷The LORD of hosts is with us;
>   The God of Jacob is our stronghold. Selah.
> ⁸Come, behold the works of the LORD,
>   Who has wrought desolations in the earth.
> ⁹He makes wars to cease to the end of the earth;
>   He breaks the bow and cuts the spear in two;
>   He burns the chariots with fire.
> ¹⁰"Cease striving and know that I am God;
>   I will be exalted among the nations, I will be exalted in the earth."
> ¹¹The LORD of hosts is with us;
>   The God of Jacob is our stronghold. Selah.

Ps. 46

God is our refuge and strength (v. 1)

God is our "refuge," which means that He is a place of shelter, a place of safety. He is the One to whom we must run, just as a young child runs from a deadly snake to its mother. His are the shoulders upon which we must learn to cry when we are overcome with grief and pain. The Bible presents many other images of the surety of God's loving care for us in times of fear and sorrow. The following are just a few.

Moses paints a picture of strong, loving care when he writes, "The eternal God is a dwelling place, and underneath are the everlasting arms" (Deut. 33:27). The descriptive words "everlasting arms" illustrate the Creator's strong protection and tender care on our behalf. Another image that helps us appreciate the attention God gives His children is the Scripture's use of "wings." When David fled from Saul, he prayed,

> Be gracious to me, O God, be gracious to me,
>   For my soul takes refuge in You;
>   And in the shadow of Your wings I will take refuge
>   Until destruction passes by.
>
> Ps. 57:1

Moses also made use of this image in Psalm 91:4:

> He will cover you with His pinions [outer edges of a bird's wing]
>   And under His wings you may seek refuge;
>   His faithfulness is a shield and bulwark.

Like a protective mother bird, God spreads out His wings of love to guard His children so that "No evil will befall [them]" (Ps. 91:10). However, we must receive this protection by faith, as illustrated by Jesus' words: "Jerusalem, Jerusalem, who kills the prophets and stones those who are sent to her! How often I wanted to gather your children together, the way a hen gathers her chicks under her wings, and you were unwilling" (Matt. 23:37).

Of course, we know that God does not have arms like a man or wings like a bird. These figures of speech are employed to remind us how much our God loves, cares, and holds us up in times of trial. He covers us with His wings to protect us from the storms of life, which are usually unpredictable. Science has the technology to keep an eye on the atmosphere, through the use of weather-tracking satellites hanging in space, but we do not have that type of alarm for spiritual and emotional storms. God simply does not warn us ahead of time. He does warn of difficulty in a general way (John 16:33; 1 Peter 4:12), but not in the particulars of our individual situations. If He did, we would easily be trained to walk by sight rather than by faith. Therefore, we need to trust Him. He is in control. When fierce storms come, we must not be ashamed to run and hide in God.

In addition to being our refuge, God is our "strength." His power is put into action for us. Knowing this, we ought to 'Seek the Lord and His strength; seek His face continually" (1 Chr. 16:11). His strength works *for us* in our time of weakness. In fact, according to the apostle Paul, the strength of God is made perfect. It is made whole in our daily experience, not when we are strong in ourselves, but when we are weak (2 Cor. 12:9). It is when we feel as if the rug has been pulled out from beneath us that we recognize just how weak we really are. Then the strength of God is made perfect, that is, complete. We experience the fullness of God's strength when we are humbled by our weakness.

He is also our "very present help" in times of sorrow and fear. In other words, His omnipresence is put into action on our behalf. God is not ever-present in a distant kind of way; He is our ever-present "help." Therefore, we share the psalmist's confidence: "The Lord is near to all who call upon Him, to all who call upon Him in truth" (Ps. 145:18). God is not near to all, but only to those who approach Him on the basis of His truth revealed in Scripture. He is near to those who realize their need to be near Him. He is near to those who run to Him as their refuge and strength. This rock-solid theological foundation leads the author of Psalm 46 to assure us of two results of hiding in God.

When God is our refuge, we have no cause to fear (vv. 2–7)

When we fear God, revere Him above anything or anyone, and place our total trust in Him, we have no cause to fear our present circumstances or the worries of the future. Because God is our refuge, "Therefore, we will not fear." The word "therefore" takes us back to verse 1. In other words, because "God is our refuge and strength, a very present help in trouble," we have no reason to fear. Proverbs 14:26 adds this security: "In the fear of the LORD there is strong confidence, and his children will have refuge." When the Lord is our refuge, we have the strength to face all our fears, even the fear of death—our own death or the death of a loved one. Jesus exhorts in Matthew 10:28, "Do not fear those who kill the body but are unable to kill the soul; but rather fear Him who is able to destroy both soul and body in hell." When our loved one returns from a visit to the cancer specialist with the news that nothing more can be done, that "it is only a matter of time," our hearts and voices may cry out in fear. But God is our refuge, "Therefore, we will not fear." Trusting God dispels all other fears because only He is sovereign over death. As we grow in our love for God, this "perfect love casts out fear" (1 John 4:18).

The psalmist reveals two situations which often produce fear.

When circumstances are beyond our control (vv. 2–5)
Fear may be defined as misplaced trust. That is, instead of trusting God, we trust something else. Often it is ourselves in whom we place our trust. We trust our ability to control our own destiny, circumstances, or immediate future. We don't like not being able to control events in our lives, especially the causes of devastating news that awake us to the reality of our human frailty. So we worry, because we fear the loss of control. But

faith is a positive loss of control, a relinquishing of our supposed authority over our lives, a willing surrender of our control to God, who possesses ultimate control as well as infinite goodness and wisdom. In an excellent book on suffering, Dustin Shramek gives this vivid illustration of faith that clings to God especially when we do not feel we have the strength to hang on:

> Experiencing grief and pain is like falling off a cliff. Everything has been turned upside down, and we are no longer in control. As we fall, we see one *and only one* tree that is growing out from the rock face. So we grab hold of it and cling to it with all our might. This tree is our holy God. He alone can keep us from falling headfirst to our doom. There simply aren't any other trees to grab. So we cling to this tree (the holy God) with all our might. But what we didn't realize is that when we fell and grabbed the tree our arm actually became entangled in the branches, so that in reality, the tree is holding us. We hold on to keep from falling, but what we don't realize is that we can't fall because the tree has us. We are safe. God, in his holiness, is keeping us and showing mercy to us. We may not be aware of it, but it is true. He is with us even in the deepest and darkest pit.[3]

When circumstances are beyond our control and seem to be working against us, we must hold on to the truth that God loves us and that there is nothing that can separate us from that love if we are in Christ. "For I am convinced that neither death, nor life, nor angels, nor principalities, nor things present, nor things to come, nor powers, nor height, nor depth, nor any other created thing, will be able to separate us from the love of God, which is in Christ Jesus our Lord" (Rom. 8:38–39). God is not a generic refuge for every person on earth, but only for those who belong to Him by repentant faith in Jesus Christ.

Mankind consists of two categories: children of God and

children of the devil (1 John 3:10). Only children of God have the impenetrable assurance of God's covenant love in any and every trial of life. John 1:11–13 says of Christ:

> He came to His own, and those who were His
> own did not receive Him. But as many as received
> Him, to them He gave the right to become children
> of God, even to those who believe in His name,
> who were born, not of blood nor of the will of
> the flesh nor of the will of man, but of God.

In other words, we are not children of God by physical birth, but by the new birth, by faith in Jesus Christ, by the spiritual rebirth brought about by the Spirit of God (John 3:1–8).

When we have assurance of a relationship with God through His Son, we possess a refuge in Him. The psalmist continues: even "though the earth should change," or "mountains slip into the heart of the sea," "though its waters roar and foam," and the "mountains quake," we will not fear. Why? Because the living God, our refuge and strength, is present with us. Again, the causes of fear mentioned by the psalmist are totally beyond our control. We have no control over earthquakes or mountains slipping into the sea. God alone controls these things. We must remember that, no matter how difficult our circumstances may become, we are never alone. God is our very present help. The psalmist is saying, "Trust God. Fear God, and nothing else."

To fear God is to escape from all other fears, to anchor our souls to an immovable rock in a harbor of strong defense. When I struggle with fear, I will often drive a few miles to the shore of Lake Michigan, one of the Great Lakes, to look at the waves and reflect on the awesome power of God. Though the waves sometimes rage, threatening to damage the docked sailboats and yachts, the water in the harbor is calm because of the protection of the breakwater. The boats that rest in the harbor are quiet; they are secure, because the rock wall is designed to hold back the threatening waves. Using the same imagery, James Bruce writes of the painful waves of grief:

> Real grief is not easily comforted. It comes like ocean waves rushing up the sand, subsiding back, only to roll in again. These waves vary in size, frequency, and intensity. Some are small, lapping up around the feet. Others are stronger; they foam the water around you and cause you to stagger. Then there are the overwhelming waves with an under-tow that can turn your world upside down and drag you out into deep waters. In times such as those, the mourner desperately needs an anchor.[4]

That anchor is God. He is our refuge and strength. As long as we trust in Him, we remain unshakeable, safe, and secure in His tender care.

No matter how difficult our storms may be, we can endure them with inner calm and joy. "There is a river whose streams make glad the city of God, the holy dwelling places of the Most High" (v. 4). Again, we are assured of the Lord's omnipresence: "God is in the midst of her, she will not be moved; God will help her when morning dawns" (v. 5). It is peaceful in the city of God, where He dwells. When circumstances are beyond our control, we are exactly where God wants us to be so that we learn to trust Him who delights in coming to our aid.

When opposition arises before us (vv. 6–7)
We are safe in God's care not only when the circumstances of life are beyond our control, but also when we face opposition from God's enemies. Though "The nations made an uproar, the kingdoms tottered," "He raised His voice, the earth melted" (v. 6). When God speaks, His enemies are forced to flee. When all the nations of the earth stand to oppose the Lord of heaven, He will simply open His mouth and they will be destroyed (Rev. 19:15). When Jesus faced the temptations of

Satan, He simply spoke forth the Word of God and "the devil left Him" (Matt. 4:11).

The same is true when we face spiritual opposition. When the enemy attacks our faith, we rest in the truth that "The LORD of hosts is with us; the God of Jacob is our stronghold" (v. 7). This is the hymn-writer's confidence: "Though sorrows befall us and Satan oppose ... through grace we can conquer, defeat all our foes." When God is our refuge, we have no cause to fear, because "God leads His dear children along."[5] As children of God, there is nothing to fear because He has a plan for us. He will lead us along the path, holding our hand, no matter what the future may hold. God is our refuge. He is our strength. He is our safety. There is no reason to fear.

WHEN GOD IS OUR REFUGE, WE HAVE NO CAUSE TO FRET (VV. 8–11)

In light of this assurance of God's protection, we must also "Cease striving" (v. 10). This is the second lesson of this psalm. The Hebrew word translated "cease" means to sink, or relax; and "striving" is actually a term referring to warfare. So the admonition is basically this: "Be at peace."

According to Philippians 4:6–7, the God-given means of gaining this protective peace is prayer: "Be anxious for nothing [do not fret], but in everything by prayer and supplication with thanksgiving let your requests be made known to God. And the peace of God, which surpasses all comprehension, will guard your hearts and your minds in Christ Jesus." When we bring our fears and worries to God in prayer, He sends His peace to stand like a sentry at the doors of our hearts and our minds, securing a deadbolt against anxiety.

Remembering the powerful deeds of God is also an essential weapon in the battle against fear. Verses 8 to 10 instruct us,

> Come, behold the works of the LORD,
>   Who has wrought desolations in the earth.
> He makes wars to cease to the end of the earth;

31

> He breaks the bow and cuts the spear in two;
> He burns the chariots with fire.
> "Cease striving and know that I am God."

In other words, "Stop worrying! I am God—you are not! I will get the victory. Stop acting as if you are in charge. Stop, relax, rest in Me. I am your God. I will be your peace."

This spiritual rest is not passive, but is a demonstration of active faith. Concerning the comforting rest found in God, Walter Kaiser writes, "The word for 'rest' (*manoah*) is related in Hebrew to the word for 'comfort' (*menahem*) and is a word possessing considerable theological weight. The 'rest' of God is *a state of being that we enter into by belief* [emphasis added]."[6] In other words, resting in God actually requires an active choice to stop worrying and instead believe that God is God and is, therefore, in full control. As fears threaten to overtake us and destroy our peace, we must rest in God by faith. The psalmist gives three reasons not to fret.

Because God's works are powerful (vv. 8–9)
The first reason not to fret is because God is all-powerful. We need to remember His mighty deeds: "Come, behold the works of the LORD." When we are tempted to worry, we must remember the great works that God has done—not only in the earth, but in our own lives. We must reflect on the many ways in which He has providentially cared for us, satisfied our needs, and demonstrated His power, love, and grace. This is an antidote to worry. It is the same principle Jesus taught His disciples in Matthew 6:25–34:

> For this reason [because you cannot serve two masters]
> I say to you, do not be worried about your life, as to
> what you will eat, or what you will drink; nor for your
> body, as to what you will put on. Is not life more than
> food, and the body more than clothing? Look at the
> birds of the air [behold the works of God!], that they do

not sow, nor reap, nor gather into barns, and yet your heavenly Father feeds them. Are you not worth much more than they? And who of you by being worried can add a single hour to his life? And why are you worried about clothing? Observe how the lilies of the field grow [behold the works of God!]; they do not toil nor do they spin, yet I say to you that not even Solomon in all his glory clothed himself like one of these. But if God so clothes the grass of the field [behold the works of God!], which is alive today and tomorrow is thrown into the furnace, will He not much more clothe you? You of little faith! Do not worry then, saying, "What will we eat?" or "What will we drink?" or "What will we wear for clothing?" For the Gentiles eagerly seek all these things; for your heavenly Father knows that you need all these things. But seek first His kingdom and His righteousness; and all these things will be added to you. So do not worry about tomorrow; for tomorrow will care for itself. Each day has enough trouble of its own.

Worry hinders our faith as it clouds our focus, robbing us of our ability to see clearly the good works of the Lord and, as a result, bringing no benefit. Someone has well said, "Worry is like a rocking chair. It will give you something to do, but it won't get you anywhere."[7] Worry is also an enemy of faith. Instead of fretting over that which we cannot control, we must learn to quietly rest in the One who is sovereign over every atom in the universe. Jesus Christ, the omnipotent Creator, "is before all things, and in Him all things hold together" (Col. 1:17).

Because God's will is unshakable (v. 10)
The second reason the psalmist gives for not fretting is because the will of God cannot be thwarted: "I will be exalted among the nations, I will be exalted in the earth" (v. 10). When God says, "I will," mark it down; it will happen. His will is unshakable.

Therefore, we should not fret about what God is doing in our lives, but rather accept that He is working out His good and perfect will through our grief and pain in order to bring His plan to completion. "And we know that God causes all things to work together for good to those who love God, to those who are called according to His purpose. For those whom He foreknew, He also predestined to become conformed to the image of His Son" (Rom. 8:28–29). His unshakable will is to make us more like Christ—and He will stop at nothing to accomplish it. He is working in, behind, and through all the events of our lives in order to accomplish what is for our good and to magnify His glory as we are progressively shaped into the image of His Son.

Because God's presence is real (v. 11)
The third reason not to fret is because of the attentive presence of God in the lives of His children. Verse 11 repeats a key truth: "The LORD of hosts is with us; the God of Jacob is our stronghold." This sentence was already stated in verse 7 and, in a sense, also in verse 1, but in different words: "God is … a very present help in trouble." By stating the same truth three times, the psalmist is making a point that we must never forget when we are in the midst of our storms: God's presence is real. He is not far away; He is very near.

Do you trust this God? Jesus says that He will never leave you nor forsake you. Never! Never will He leave you. Never will He forsake you. No matter how painful your trial may become, God will always remain with you if you belong to Him in Christ. This truth is beautifully communicated in a poem based on Isaiah 43:2 and entitled "When Thou Passest Through the Waters." May it encourage you as it has me.

> Is there any heart discouraged as it journeys on its way?
> Does there seem to be more darkness than there is of
>   sunny day?

Oh, it's hard to learn the lesson, as we pass beneath
    the rod,
That the sunshine and the shadow serve alike the will
    of God;
But there comes a world of promise like the promise in
    the bow—
That however deep the waters, they shall never
    overflow.

When the flesh is worn and weary, and the spirit is
    depressed,
And temptations sweep upon it, like a storm on
    ocean's breast,
There's a haven ever open for the tempest-driven bird;
There's a shelter for the tempted in the promise of
    the Word;
For the standard of the Spirit shall be raised against
    the foe,
And however deep the waters, they shall never overflow.

When a sorrow comes upon you that no other soul
    can share,
And the burden seems too heavy for the human heart
    to bear,
There is One whose grace can comfort if you'll give
    Him an abode;
There's a Burden-Bearer ready if you'll trust Him with
    your load;
For the precious promise reaches to the depth of
    human woe,
That however deep the waters, they shall never
    overflow.

When the sands of life are ebbing and I know that death
 is near;
When I'm passing through the valley, and the way seems
 dark and drear;
I will reach my hand to Jesus, in His bosom I shall hide,
And 'twill only be a moment till I reach the other side;
It is then the fullest meaning of the promise I shall
 know.
"When thou passest through the waters, they shall
 never overflow."[8]

Let us pray.

*Father, we thank You for this promise because the waters of
life are sometimes very deep—deeper than we ever expected.
And yet, when the storms of life come upon us, Your Word gives
us so many promises. When You cause us to pass through deep
waters, they will never overflow. They will never go beyond the
barrier that You have set for them. You are the one who says
to them, "You may come this far and no further." You hold
us in the palm of Your hand. In Christ, we are Your children.
You have made a commitment to us and will care for us. You
will never leave us nor forsake us. Oh, what a great promise!
Minister to all of our hearts. May we run and hide in You—in
the refuge, the shelter in our time of storm. We love you, Lord,
because You first loved us. May You fill our hearts with the kind
of faith and simple childlike trust that the psalmist spoke of, so
that we will walk with You in peace and joy. And may the world
look upon us and be baffled by the inner peace that we have
because we know You. May we be a bright light in our storms
for the glory and honor of Jesus Christ, the One who has made
it all possible. In His name we pray. Amen.*

Musical
comfort

Chapter 2

Nothing comforts me more in my greatest
sufferings, nor seems more fit for me while I wait for
death, than singing psalms of praise to God, nor is
there any exercise in which I had rather end my life.

–Richard Baxter[1]

Without doubt, music plays a large part in life's celebrations, but nothing matches its ability to touch the deepest parts of our inner person as it comforts us in the midst of our grief and pain. The above words from the Puritan pastor Richard Baxter remind us of the power of music to soothe our troubled souls and to strengthen us to face the trials of life—even death itself—with God-centered confidence.

No doubt the most vivid biblical example of the power of music to minister to the inner man is the effect that David's music had on King Saul. First Samuel 16:23 testifies, "So it came about whenever the evil spirit from God came to Saul, David would take the harp and play it with his hand; and Saul would be refreshed and be well, and the evil spirit would depart from him." Setting aside any discussion regarding the place of demonic influence in Saul's life, or the role that godly music may have in dispelling the forces of darkness, it serves us well to consider here the fact that it was the music itself that ministered to the king, causing him to "be refreshed and be well."

Since the Bible, the Word of God, is the revelation of God to man (Ps. 19:7–10), divine truth (John 17:17), and the mind of God in written form (1 Cor. 2:16), it is the chief instrument that the Holy Spirit uses to comfort us. Therefore, there is not a more powerful musical comforter than the spiritual songs and great hymns of the faith that forever wed biblical truths to memorable melodies. What believer has not had emotions spring up within when "It Is Well with My Soul" (Horatio G. Spafford) was sung at his or her deepest moment of sorrow? Who has not been moved to tears when "Face to Face" (Carrie E. Breck) was sung at the memorial service of a devoted follower of Jesus? When the promises of God are conveyed through the beauty of God's musical creation, profound ministry takes place in the souls of men and women.

There is also great benefit to the use of hymn stories. Often the circumstances in the life of the hymn-writer will mirror those that threaten the faith of hurting believers today. Sharing these stories will bring other empathetic comforters to their aid. Therefore, we should make use of the many excellent hymn-story books that are available.[2] All in all, we are foolish if we do not avail ourselves of the rich hymnody that God has preserved in His church for the purpose of glorifying Himself and comforting His people.

A sermon outline for a hymn meditation on "Be Still, My Soul"

"Be Still, My Soul" has been used by God to minister to His people in times of grief for nearly 300 years. Countless believers have undoubtedly been helped by the verses of this hymn and, more importantly, the biblical truths that the verses were based upon. The hymn's scriptural launching point is Psalm 46:10, "Be still, and know that I am God" (KJV), but the lyrics speak well of the entire psalm, expounded in the previous chapter.

"Be Still, My Soul" was written by a German woman named Katharina von Schlegel, who lived from 1697 to about 1768. It is hard to imagine church life without congregational singing, but for some reason this important part of public worship was lost during the latter part of the 17th century. Thankfully, it was rediscovered when a new movement of evangelism, known as the Pietistic revival, began in Germany, a movement similar to the Puritan and Wesleyan movements in England. One author commenting on the origin of this hymn writes, "A pastor of a Lutheran church in Berlin, Philipp Jacob Spener, was the leader of this German movement. He was not a hymn-writer himself but greatly encouraged singing which provided immense hymnody revival in Germany during that time. The hymns from this movement were characterized by profound and rich Christian experience, genuine piety, and faithfulness to the Scriptures."[3] As a result of the movement of the Spirit of God in this and other revivals, today's church owns a treasury of great music that continues to minister to the deepest needs of the soul.

Not much is known about Katharina von Schlegel except that she was a Lutheran and was probably of aristocratic birth, because of the "von" in her name. She contributed lyrics to a number of other songs, but this is her most famous hymn. The original version contained at least six verses, but most hymnals include only three. Approximately 100 years after it was written, "Be Still, My Soul" was translated into English by Jane L. Borthwick, a devoted religious and social worker in the Free Church of Scotland.

"Be Still, My Soul" calls us as believers to apply Psalm 46:10 to the troubles that we experience in our lives. Six times the hymn-writer exhorts us to be still and know that God is God. She bids us to settle down and be quiet. However, von Schlegel not only exhorts us, but in a very real sense she also talks to herself. She is telling herself to be still, to quiet down, and to remember that God is God and she is not. We must do the same.

> Be still, my soul: the Lord is on thy side;
> Bear patiently the cross of grief or pain.
> Leave to Thy God to order and provide;
> In every change He faithful will remain.
> Be still, my soul: thy best, thy heav'nly Friend
> Thro' thorny ways leads to a joyful end.
>
> Be still, my soul: thy God doth undertake
> To guide the future as He has the past.

> Thy hope, thy confidence let nothing shake;
> All now mysterious shall be bright at last.
> Be still, my soul: the waves and winds still know
> His voice Who ruled them while He dwelt below.
>
> Be still, my soul: the hour is hast'ning on
> When we shall be forever with the Lord,
> When disappointment, grief, and fear are gone,
> Sorrow forgot, love's purest joys restored.
> Be still, my soul: when change and tears are past,
> All safe and blessèd we shall meet at last.[4]

Each verse contains a theme that is developed and explained by three pairs of phrases. Below is an outline of the hymn that could be used as the basis of a sermon. Selected Scriptures are listed for the pastor to expound throughout the message in order to bring the promises of God as the means of His comfort to the forefront of believers' minds.

Introduction

Give a brief overview of Psalm 46, with special attention given to verse 10: "Be still, and know that I am God" (KJV).

Rest in the faithful God (hymn verse 1)

Three reasons are given:

HE IS FOR US

> Be still, my soul: the Lord is on thy side;
> Bear patiently the cross of grief or pain.

Romans 8:28–31

HIS PLAN IS WISE

> Leave to Thy God to order and provide;
> In every change He faithful will remain.

Psalm 37:1–5, 23
Lamentations 3:21–23

HE IS OUR JOY

> Be still, my soul: thy best, thy heav'nly Friend
> Thro' thorny ways leads to a joyful end.

Philippians 3:13–14
Philippians 1:21

Rely on the sovereign God (v. 2)

Three reasons are given:

HE IS OVER ALL OUR DAYS

> Be still, my soul: thy God doth undertake
> To guide the future as He has the past.

Psalm 139:16
Proverbs 3:5–6

HE IS OVER THE HIDDEN THINGS

> Thy hope, thy confidence let nothing shake;
> All now mysterious shall be bright at last.

1 Corinthians 4:1–5

HE IS OVER ALL OF NATURE

> Be still, my soul: the waves and winds still know
> His voice Who ruled them while He dwelt below.

Mark 4:35–41
Psalm 135:6–7

Remember his heavenly promise (v. 3)

Three reasons are given:

THE PROMISE INCLUDES ETERNAL FELLOWSHIP

> Be still, my soul: the hour is hast'ning on
> When we shall be forever with the Lord …

2 Corinthians 5:6–8

THE PROMISE INCLUDES PURE HAPPINESS

> When disappointment, grief, and fear are gone,
> Sorrow forgot, love's purest joys restored.

Revelation 21:1–6
Romans 8:18

THE PROMISE INCLUDES BLESSED REUNION (WITH BELIEVERS WHO'VE GONE BEFORE US)
> Be still, my soul: when change and tears are past,
> All safe and blessèd we shall meet at last.

1 Thessalonians 4:13–18

Conclusion
Use Psalm 37:7 to wrap up your thoughts on the comfort of God.

God's delight in the death of a believer

Chapter 3

It is not death to die,
To leave this weary road,
And midst the brotherhood on high
To be at home with God ...
... Jesus, Thou Prince of Life,
Thy chosen cannot die;
Like Thee, they conquer in the strife
To reign with Thee on high.

–H. A. Cesar Malan[1]

The death of a church member is a difficult experience for the entire church body. Scripture teaches that "there are many members, but one body" (1 Cor. 12:20). Like each part of the human body, each member of the church needs all the other parts for the church's proper health and function: "And the eye cannot say to the hand, 'I have no need of you'; or again the head to the feet, 'I have no need of you'" (1 Cor. 12:21). The reality of this interdependence is especially felt when one or more members are in the midst of deep suffering. This mutual experience of grief within a church is not a sign of weakness, but an indicator that the church is functioning exactly as God designed it to function. For "if one member suffers, all the members suffer with it" (1 Cor. 12:26). Therefore, a pastor must be sensitive to the needs of the flock that God has called him to shepherd. He must be ready at a moment's notice to shift gears in his preaching in order to address what he already knows preoccupies the minds of the sheep.

This chapter contains the transcript of a sermon I preached at my church on April 13, 2008, the morning after Jean Pitz went home to be with the Lord. When this sister passed into eternity, her pastors and family members surrounded her bed singing "It Is Well with My Soul" (Horatio G. Spafford). When she took her last breath, I immediately knew that I could not step into the pulpit the next morning and continue preaching where I had left off the Sunday before. The heart-needs of my flock were very evident and very specific. They had wounds that needed to be tended by their shepherd. This sermon has only been modified slightly for publication and, therefore, serves as an example of how a pastor may use the Word of God to dispense God's grace in a time of deep loss.

Last summer, on July 8, 2007, I preached a sermon very much like this one during the evening service. Our limited knowledge pointed to Jean's imminent death. Everything we knew pointed to it. Everything the doctors knew pointed to it. But God's people prayed. We called upon the Lord. We pleaded with Him. We had all-night prayer vigils for our dear sister who had brought spiritual encouragement into all of our lives. And God answered. He raised up Jean to the bewilderment of the medical establishment. And He gave her back to us for nine more months. He gave her family one more Thanksgiving, Christmas, and Easter together. He gave all of us the honor of serving her and walking through the dark valley of cancer with her. And she walked this way with joy. She did it with peace that can only be explained by the salvation that Jesus purchased for her. And then God determined to bring her home to share His eternal peace, rest, and joy. He did this last night at 7:30 p.m., and we are grieving. But it is not wrong to grieve.

The Bible contains many examples of human grief. Abraham grieved the death of Sarah, his wife. Genesis 23:2 says, "Sarah died in Kiriath-arba (that is, Hebron) in the land of Canaan; and Abraham went in to mourn for Sarah and to weep for her." The New Testament reveals that godly men grieved the death of Stephen: "Some devout men buried Stephen, and made loud lamentation over him" (Acts 8:2). In the next chapter of the book of Acts, we read of widows grieving the death of Dorcas, a godly servant. As they wept over their loss, they also remembered her service to the church. Acts 9:39 describes the scene: "So Peter arose and went with them. When he arrived, they brought him into the upper room; and all the widows stood beside him, weeping and showing all the tunics and garments that Dorcas used to make while she was with them." Even Jesus, the Son of God, grieved the death of his good friend Lazarus. John 11:33–36 says, "When Jesus therefore saw her [Mary] weeping, and the Jews who came with her also weeping, He was deeply moved in spirit and was troubled, and said, 'Where have you laid him?' They said to Him, 'Lord, come and see.' Jesus wept. So the Jews were saying, 'See how He loved him!'" The apostle Paul also grieved as he anticipated the death of Epaphroditus, a fellow worker in the Lord. He wrote to the church in Philippi, "For indeed he was sick to the point of death, but God had mercy on him, and not on him only but also on me, so that I would not have sorrow upon sorrow" (Phil. 2:27).

These examples of sorrow testify to the reality that grief is part of the human experience and part of being created in God's image. The Father grieved the wickedness of pre-flood humanity (Gen. 6:6); Jesus, the sinless Son of God, grieved (as noted above); and the Holy Spirit grieves when believers sin against one another (Eph. 4:30). Made in God's image, we are emotional creatures, and, therefore, we also grieve.

However, there is another truth in the Scriptures that we must bring to the forefront of our minds: God delights in the death of a believer. In Psalm 116:15, we read these words: "Precious in the sight of the LORD is the death of His godly ones." Although death is a result of the curse of sin (Gen. 2:17) and is our enemy (1 Cor. 15:26), God does not view the death of a believer as a bad thing. Rather, He considers it precious. John affirms this in Revelation 14:13: "And I heard a voice from heaven, saying, 'Write, "Blessed are the dead who die in the Lord from now on!"'"

49

'Yes,' says the Spirit, 'so that they may rest from their labors, for their deeds follow with them.'" In light of this truth, there are two questions that arise in my mind and perhaps in yours: Why is the death of a believer precious to God? And why does the Bible present the death of a believer as a good and positive event when it is so painful to us? Let's look at the answers to these important questions.

The death of a believer employs the ministry of God's comfort

In 2 Corinthians 1:3–7 we read,

> Blessed be the God and Father of our Lord Jesus
> Christ, the Father of mercies and God of all comfort,
> who comforts us in all our affliction so that we will be
> able to comfort those who are in any affliction with
> the comfort with which we ourselves are comforted
> by God. For just as the sufferings of Christ are ours in
> abundance, so also our comfort is abundant through
> Christ. But if we are afflicted, it is for your comfort and
> salvation; or if we are comforted, it is for your comfort,
> which is effective in the patient enduring of the same
> sufferings which we also suffer; and our hope for you
> is firmly grounded, knowing that as you are sharers of
> our sufferings, so also you are sharers of our comfort.

When we grieve, our attention needs to be intentionally drawn to God, which is exactly what Paul does when he calls God "the Father of mercies and God of all comfort." In other words, there is no mercy in this life that does not come from the Father. There is no comfort that does not ultimately come from God. He is the God of *all* comfort. And He comforts us *in* all our affliction— in the midst of our grief and pain, God comes to our aid. In suffering, we experience the comfort of God in a deeper way than could ever be experienced if our lives were free of anguish and affliction.

The purpose for which He comforts us is so that we may comfort others. Verse 4 says that God comforts us "so that [here's the purpose] we will be able to comfort those who are in any affliction with the comfort with which we ourselves are comforted by God." God comforts us in the midst of our affliction so that we will be better equipped to comfort others. Through Jean's death, the Lord is sharing His comfort with us so that in the days ahead we might share it with others who will need it in the future. Lest believers think this is strange, Paul says, "For just as the sufferings of Christ are ours in abundance, so also our comfort is abundant through Christ" (v. 5). As we suffer with Jesus, we are also comforted with Him.

Another Scripture that illustrates this same principle is 1 Thessalonians 4:13–18. Here Paul teaches that the death of a believer employs God's comfort by reminding us of the return of Jesus Christ. The letter that we know as 1 Thessalonians was written partly because the believers were confused concerning prophetic events. By correcting their theology of the end times, Paul brought God's comfort to them.

> But we do not want you to be uninformed, brethren, about those who are asleep, so that you will not grieve as do the rest who have no hope [believers grieve, but they do so differently from unbelievers]. For if we believe that Jesus died and rose again, even so God will bring with Him those who have fallen asleep in Jesus. For this we say to you by the word of the Lord, that we who are alive and remain until the coming of the Lord, will not precede those who have fallen asleep. For the Lord Himself will descend from heaven with a shout, with the voice of the archangel and with the trumpet of God, and the dead in Christ will rise first. Then we

who are alive and remain will be caught up together
with them in the clouds to meet the Lord in the air, and
so we shall always be with the Lord. Therefore *comfort
one another with these words* [emphasis added].

Paul writes in order to comfort believers who did not know
what would happen to other Christians who had already died.
"The dead in Christ will rise first"; in other words, if we are
alive on this earth when Jesus returns, then Jean will precede us.
That is, the resurrection of Jean's body will precede our rapture,
but we will meet her in the air. Paul essentially says, "Don't
worry. God will be faithful in caring for those who have died in
Christ before us. They are secure in Him. Be sure to comfort one
another with these truths."

The death of a believer exalts the infinite value of knowing Jesus Christ

In Philippians 1:19–20 we read these words:

… for I know that this [my imprisonment]will
turn out for my deliverance through your prayers
and the provision of the Spirit of Jesus Christ,
according to my earnest expectation and hope, that
I will not be put to shame in anything, but that with
all boldness, Christ will even now, as always, be
exalted in my body, whether by life or by death.

Paul is convinced that he belongs to Jesus Christ and, therefore,
that His Lord will be exalted whether he lives or whether he
dies. His classic statement "For to me, to live is Christ and to die
is gain" (v. 21) verbalizes his conviction that to live is to know
Christ, to walk with Christ, to be in fellowship with Him, and to
serve Him. Paul says that is what it means to live. "If I can't do
that, then why live?" is essentially what he is saying. Paul viewed
death as spiritual gain because he knew that, frightening as the
process might be, it was the vehicle that would immediately

bring him into the real presence of the Lord whom he loved and served.

He continues in verses 22–24:

> But if I am to live on in the flesh, this will mean
> fruitful labor for me; and I do not know which
> to choose. But I am hard-pressed from both
> directions, having the desire to depart and be with
> Christ, for that is very much better; yet to remain
> on in the flesh is more necessary for your sake.

Paul was caught between a rock and a hard place. He loved Christ and he loved serving Him. Yet he knew that the moment he died, he would be with his Lord; he would gain Him. He was squeezed from both directions. Part of him wanted to stay here and serve Christ with all of his heart, and part of him wanted to go and be with His Savior immediately. He knew that, if his earthly life continued, it was for the sake of other believers. As Christians, we need to have the same mindset. Whatever time God gives us here on earth should be used to serve others in His name.

Later, in the same book, Paul reveals his heart's passion: "that I may know Him and the power of His resurrection and the fellowship of His sufferings, being conformed to His death" (3:10). Paul was driven to know Christ even if it required the experience of death. Since death leads to the consummation of the believer's relationship with the Savior, it is not the end. Death is a new beginning in the presence of the Savior who died for us. That is *life*, not death. First John 3:2 testifies, "Beloved, now we are children of God, and it has not appeared as yet what we will be. We know that when He appears, we will be like Him, because we will see Him just as He is." This is our hope! The moment we see Jesus, whether by death or by rapture, we shall be like Him. Therefore, we can rejoice in the midst of our grief.

The death of a believer engenders anticipation for the fullness of redemption

The third answer to our questions is that the death of a believer builds in our hearts an anticipation of the redemption that belongs to us in Jesus. The death of a believer produces a longing for the completion of what God has begun (Phil. 1:6). This is Paul's point in 2 Corinthians 5:1–8:

> For we know that if the earthly tent which is our house [the human body that houses who we really are] is torn down, we have a building from God [the glorified body of the believer], a house not made with hands, eternal in the heavens. For indeed in this house we groan, longing to be clothed with our dwelling from heaven, inasmuch as we, having put it on, will not be found naked.
> For indeed while we are in this tent, we groan, being burdened, because we do not want to be unclothed, but to be clothed, so that what is mortal will be swallowed up by life. Now He who prepared us for this very purpose is God, who gave to us the Spirit as a pledge. Therefore, being always of good courage, and knowing that while we are at home in the body we are absent from the Lord—for we walk by faith, not by sight—we are of good courage, I say, and prefer rather to be absent from the body and to be at home with the Lord.

Here Paul looks forward to the fullness of his redemption. When he speaks of the earthly tent (the human body that is already in the process of decaying, even while we live), his heart fills with anticipation. While here, we groan; we are burdened. Yet we know that the Holy Spirit has been given to us as a pledge: a down payment, the promise of something more to come, which is the resurrection—at which time our mortal bodies will be "swallowed up by life" (v. 4). When our bodies are raised from the grave, we shall receive new ones—glorified bodies—that will not be susceptible to cancer, strokes, or heart disease. They will never die again, but will house our spirits for all eternity.

In that great resurrection chapter, 1 Corinthians 15, Paul writes, "The last enemy that will be abolished is death" (v. 26). When Jesus rose from the grave on the first day of the week, He secured our resurrection. He is "the first fruits of those who are asleep" (v. 20), meaning that His resurrection is the guarantee of more to come. At the final resurrection, death will be forever destroyed. Until then, death seeks to threaten us. Paul Tripp writes,

> We all feel death's wrenching finality. Death is so wrong, so completely out of step with life as God planned it. The apostle Paul could think of no better word for it than "enemy" (1 Cor. 15:25–26). Death is the enemy of everything good and beautiful about life … Death was simply not meant to be. When you recognize this, you will hunger for the complete restoration of all things. You will long to live with the Lord in a place where the last enemy—death—has been defeated.[2]

The glorified bodies of believers will one day be rejoined with their spirits that are now with Christ. Body and soul together will then spend eternity with the Lord in heaven.

God is using the sorrow of this death in our congregation to produce in us a hunger for the restoration of all things to the glory of Christ. Our hope as believers is not bound to the things of this earth, not even to those we love the most. "Ours", writes Charles Spurgeon in a sermon entitled "The Hope Laid Up in Heaven," "is a hope which demands nothing of time or earth but seeks its all in the world to come."[3] One application of this truth is that we need to learn to live every day in light of the imminent return of Jesus our Lord, which will usher in the final restoration of all things. First Corinthians 15:50–58 says,

> Now I say this, brethren, that flesh and blood cannot

inherit the kingdom of God; nor does the perishable inherit the imperishable. Behold, I tell you a mystery; we will not all sleep, but we will all be changed, in a moment, in the twinkling of an eye, at the last trumpet; for the trumpet will sound, and the dead will be raised imperishable, and we will be changed. For this perishable must put on the imperishable, and this mortal must put on immortality. But when this perishable will have put on the imperishable, and this mortal will have put on immortality, then will come about the saying that is written, "Death is swallowed up in victory. O death, where is your victory? O death, where is your sting?" The sting of death is sin, and the power of sin is the law; but thanks be to God, who gives us the victory through our Lord Jesus Christ. Therefore, my beloved brethren, be steadfast, immovable, always abounding in the work of the Lord, knowing that your toil is not in vain in the Lord.

When Jesus comes, He will open every grave and raise every person, unbelievers as well as believers. Unbelievers will be raised to face the Judge of heaven at the great white throne (Rev. 20:11–15). However, the bodies of believers will be raised and reunited with their spirits that are already in the presence of God in order to spend eternity with Him in the new heaven and on the new earth. We find a description of these places in the book of Revelation.

Then I saw a new heaven and a new earth; for the first heaven and the first earth passed away, and there is no longer any sea. And I saw the holy city, new Jerusalem, coming down out of heaven from God, made ready as a bride adorned for her husband … Then one of the seven angels who had the seven bowls full of the seven last plagues came and spoke with me, saying, "Come

here, I will show you the bride, the wife of the Lamb."
And he carried me away in the Spirit to a great and high
mountain, and showed me the holy city, Jerusalem,
coming down out of heaven from God, having the glory
of God. Her brilliance was like a very costly stone, as a
stone of crystal-clear jasper ... The one who spoke with
me had a gold measuring rod to measure the city, and its
gates and its wall. The city is laid out as a square, and its
length is as great as the width; and he measured the city
with the rod, fifteen hundred miles; its length and width
and height are equal. And he measured its wall, seventy-
two yards, according to human measurements, which
are also angelic measurements. The material of the wall
was jasper; and the city was pure gold, like clear glass.
The foundation stones of the city wall were adorned
with every kind of precious stone. The first foundation
stone was jasper; the second, sapphire; the third,
chalcedony; the fourth, emerald; the fifth, sardonyx;
the sixth, sardius; the seventh, chrysolite; the eighth,
beryl; the ninth, topaz; the tenth, chrysoprase; the
eleventh, jacinth; the twelfth, amethyst. And the twelve
gates were twelve pearls; each one of the gates was a
single pearl. And the street of the city was pure gold,
like transparent glass. I saw no temple in it, for the Lord
God the Almighty and the Lamb are its temple. And the
city has no need of the sun or of the moon to shine on
it, for the glory of God has illumined it, and its lamp is
the Lamb ... Then he showed me a river of the water
of life, clear as crystal, coming from the throne of God
and of the Lamb, in the middle of its street. On either
side of the river was the tree of life, bearing twelve kinds
of fruit, yielding its fruit every month; and the leaves
of the tree were for the healing of the nations. There
will no longer be any curse; and the throne of God and

of the Lamb will be in it, and His bond-servants will serve Him; they will see His face, and His name will be on their foreheads. And there will no longer be any night; and they will not have need of the light of a lamp nor the light of the sun, because the Lord God will illumine them; and they will reign forever and ever.

Rev. 21:1–22:5

What a beautiful description of the home that awaits believers—the place where Jean now lives! "For our citizenship is in heaven, from which also we eagerly wait for a Savior, the Lord Jesus Christ; who will transform the body of our humble state into conformity with the body of His glory, by the exertion of the power that He has even to subject all things to Himself" (Phil. 3:20–21). Only a believer who has the Spirit of God living within can have the kind of eternal perspective that explains the comments that I have heard since last night. Several believers who are older than Jean have said, "I wish it was me. I wish I could trade places with Jean. I wish I was the one." Who in this world says anything like that? It is knowing Christ that gives us this hope—hope well mixed with the peace of God. Jesus says, "Peace I leave with you; My peace I give to you; not as the world gives do I give to you. Do not let your heart be troubled, nor let it be fearful" (John 14:27); and "Do not let your heart be troubled; believe in God, believe also in Me. In My Father's house are many dwelling places; if it were not so, I would have told you; for I go to prepare a place for you. If I go and prepare a place for you, I will come again and receive you to Myself, that where I am, there you may be also" (John 14:1–3).

The passage cited above from Revelation contains a promise, but the promise belongs only to those whose names are written in the Lamb's book of life. It does not belong to anyone else. So I ask you: Is your name written in the book of life? Have you repented and come to faith in Jesus Christ as your Lord and

Savior? Do you know Him? I am not asking whether you know about Him. I am not asking whether you have heard this message before. I am not asking whether or not you come to church every Sunday. I am not even asking whether you are a member of a church. I *am* asking whether you know Christ. If you don't, then this promise does not belong to you. It is not yours. Instead, there is a far more terrible, infinitely more horrible message and place that belong to you. So, come to Christ today. Do not waste another day. To know Him is life. To die knowing Him is the greatest gain.

Let us pray.

Father, we thank You and praise You for the promises in Your Word. We thank You for drawing our hearts into Your Word this morning and for causing us to reflect deeply on the eternal perspective. I pray that You will use the Word that has gone forth today to comfort, to challenge, and to save. Your Holy Spirit knows what each heart needs, so we entrust that work to You so that Christ may be glorified. In His name we pray. Amen.

Comforters-in-training: A pastoral letter to a grieving brother

Writing is not only a process of communicating with yourself as well as with others but also a way of becoming more sensitive to other human beings.

–George P. Schultz[1]

In this age of email and text messaging, the art of letter writing has almost disappeared. Yet who among us will not acknowledge the sense of love that we feel when we receive a personal letter from a caring friend? To know that our need was important enough to that person for him or her to set aside the time to write a good letter is encouraging in and of itself. But the process of writing a letter also benefits the writer, as it clarifies the thinking process. To take the thoughts that float around in our heads and skillfully arrange them on paper is a discipline that greatly improves our understanding of ourselves and what we really believe about God, and it makes us "more sensitive to other human beings," as we are forced to consider how each word may impact them.

In his Foreword to the *New York Times* bestseller *Reagan: A Life in Letters*, George Schultz says more about this discipline: "Anyone who writes knows what an effort it is to assemble your thoughts and commit them to a piece of paper. Writing is an exercise in communicating with yourself as well as with others. A good writer is almost of necessity a good thinker."[2] The process of letter writing forces us to think through the issues that impact members of our flock who are in the midst of suffering and, as a result, makes us more sensitive shepherds. In addition to our personal growth as pastors, much lasting ministry takes place through the writing of letters, as theological truths are communicated in a personal way, and can then be read over and over again. As those who serve God's people in times of loss, we need to consider making the discipline of letter writing a regular

61

part of our ministry of comfort. It is a very effective means of teaching Scripture and helping others apply its truth to life. The following is one example of this kind of letter.

Dear brother,
My heart has been aching with yours since I received the phone call about your father's death, preceded only a few weeks by your mother's. Then I think of the upheaval in your life since you suffered a stroke only six months ago. The common saying, "When it rains, it pours," is common for a reason: how true it is sometimes with God's sovereign timing of the life-changing events in our little worlds! I want you to know that I appreciate your testimony of faith in Christ and your simple trust in God during this painful time.

I've been thinking much this past week about why God ordains that these kinds of "tornadoes" pass through our lives and I want to encourage you with some biblical principles that have been simmering on the back burner of my mind. They come from two passages of Scripture. The first is Romans 8:28–29.

> And we know that God causes all things to work together for good to those who love God, to those who are called according to His purpose. For those whom He foreknew, He also predestined to become conformed to the image of His Son, so that He would be the firstborn among many brethren.

In this portion of God's Word, we see three incredible truths that apply to your current situation.

1. *All things, even bad things, are used by God to accomplish good in the lives of believers.* As a believer in Jesus Christ, you can know without a doubt that God is working out His good purpose in your life right at this moment—even if you cannot yet see it.

2. *It is God that causes all things to work toward your good.* It is not merely a "things will work out in the end" or "whatever is meant to be is meant to be" kind of fatalism. But *God is actively at work* in your life right now through this trial.

3. *The ultimate good that God is working all things in your life toward is that of shaping you into the image of Christ.* Everything that God brings into our lives is for the ultimate purpose of His glory and our good. And the best "good" for us is that we become more like Jesus. Therefore, one of the most helpful questions you can be asking right now is, "Lord, how can I become more like You *because of* these trials?"

The second Scripture passage that I want to draw your attention to is 2 Corinthians 1:2–5.

> Grace to you and peace from God our Father and
> the Lord Jesus Christ. Blessed be the God and Father
> of our Lord Jesus Christ, the Father of mercies
> and God of all comfort, who comforts us in all our
> affliction so that we will be able to comfort those
> who are in any affliction with the comfort with
> which we ourselves are comforted by God. For just
> as the sufferings of Christ are ours in abundance,
> so also our comfort is abundant through Christ.

In this passage, we see five more principles that will encourage your growth in Christ during and after your time of suffering.

1. *Grace and peace come only from God and your Lord, Jesus Christ.* Grace in time of need, and inner peace that enables you to reflect Christ in your time of trial, are two of the infinite resources that are yours in Jesus Christ. With the loss of employment due to your stroke-induced disability, you can also be confident that God will provide your every material need: "And my God will supply all your needs according to His riches in glory in Christ Jesus" (Phil. 4:19).

2. *God is the "Father of mercies and God of all comfort."* God

sees you in your present suffering through His eyes of mercy and is ready to dispense divine comfort at every moment that you need it. Indeed, He "comforts us in all our affliction."

3. *Suffering expands our ministry.* One very significant reason why God comforts us in our affliction is "so that we will be able to comfort" others who are experiencing trials. This truth greatly encouraged my wife and me when we struggled with the news of our last two daughters' deafness. We often wonder who God will bring into our lives as a result of three of our children being hearing-impaired. The same principle applies to you. There is no doubt in my mind that God is right now equipping you for future opportunities when others are afflicted in a similar way. What a joy it will be for you to be used by God in this way! We are all "comforters-in-training."

4. *Suffering authenticates our ministry.* Not only does affliction open the door to reaching more people with the hope of the gospel, but it also makes our own message of comfort more real—more believable—to those to whom we minister. We comfort others "with the comfort with which we ourselves are comforted by God." In other words, as in a relay race, we pass on to the next sufferer the same comfort that God has given to us.

5. *Both suffering and comfort are abundant in the God-centered life.* Just as Job asked his grieving wife, so we must say with contentment, "Shall we indeed accept good from God and not accept adversity?" (Job 2:10). Surely we must accept both! Increasingly, as we are conformed to the image of Christ, we will be able to accept both blessing and trial with the same gratitude and faith.

Again, I appreciate your trust in the Lord, brother, and I will continue to pray that God will use the promises in His precious Word to strengthen you in the inner man and enable you to reflect the glory of Christ to all those with whom you come into contact.

Your servant,
Pastor Paul

Part 2: Funeral meditations

I I love to preach at funerals." More than once after speaking these words I have received odd looks from people, presumably thinking that I must be some kind of morbid person. Though I am often melancholy, I do not think I am morbid. But I really do love preaching at funerals. Now, please understand: I do not like the occasion of death itself, and its accompanying grief and pain, but I am fond of the opportunity to minister to people at such a significant time in their lives, for two reasons.

First, although nothing is more radically intrusive than death, a funeral is a natural time to serve others, because their need of help and comfort is rarely made any plainer in their own sight. It becomes easier to serve people who sense the need to be served, because they more readily receive our help.

Second, although nothing is more radically intrusive than death, a funeral is an ideal time to talk about life, and death, and what comes afterward. Therefore, funerals provide a fitting platform for evangelistic preaching.

This section of the book contains four sermons that have been preached at various memorial services. Some of the characteristics will be immediately obvious. Each message strives for clarity and simplicity combined with a gentle, yet bold confrontation with the gospel. Two are very personal and tailored for the grieving family. All are intentionally evangelistic. Being so, each message assumes that there will be more than a few in the congregation who lack biblical knowledge and, therefore, "the basics" are always covered, yet not in a dumbed-down fashion. In this way, not only are unbelievers confronted with God's command to believe the gospel, but also believers in the congregation are drawn back to the purity of simple devotion to Jesus.

Bringing life out of death

Chapter 5

For Christ also died for sins once for all, the just for
the unjust, so that He might bring us to God,
having been put to death in the flesh, but made
alive in the spirit …

–1 Peter 3:18

Few things are more effective than a funeral at reminding us
that life is temporary. The purpose of a funeral is to honor
one whose earthly life has come to an end. So, death is often
viewed as the end. But that is not really the truth. Death will
teach us differently if we will stop long enough to listen. Death
will be our servant if we open our hearts to its message.

The central message of the Bible is one of hope—that the
death of one can bring life to many. You may ask, "How is that
possible? How can death bring about life?" One verse in God's
Word will answer that question. First Peter 3:18 says, "For
Christ also died for sins once for all, the just for the unjust, so
that He might bring us to God, having been put to death in the
flesh, but made alive in the spirit …" This is the truth we will
concentrate on during these brief moments we have together.
This verse tells us how God brings life out of death—how He
brings spiritual life out of the death of His only begotten Son,
Jesus Christ. Here the Son of God is described in three ways.

Christ is our sacrifice

First, Jesus Christ is our sacrifice: "For Christ also died for sins
once for all." The first three chapters of the Bible teach that God
created man from the dust of the earth and breathed into him the
breath of life. As creatures made in the image of God, man and
woman enjoyed a unique relationship which included intimate
fellowship with their Creator. God told them that this close
relationship would continue as long as they remained obedient
to His command not to eat from a certain tree in the garden. If

they disobeyed, they would surely die. However, rather than remaining obedient to God, man and woman chose to rebel against His authority. Death came as a result. Immediately, they experienced spiritual death. They knew that they were no longer at peace with God and, for that reason, hid from His presence. Physical death also entered their experience. God killed a lesser creature and made clothing out of the skins. This was the first indication that God would accept the death of one to cover the sins of another. Adam and Eve's own physical life would also surely come to an end at a later date.

Later in biblical history, God commanded a man named Abraham, the father of the Jewish nation, to offer his son as a sacrifice in order to test the loyalty of his love. Abraham obeyed, but before the knife was plunged into the boy's chest, God provided a ram to be offered as a sacrifice in place of Isaac (Gen. 22).

During the time of Moses, God delivered His people from Egyptian bondage. Before the tenth plague was brought upon the nation, God instructed His people that each household should kill a lamb and sprinkle its blood on the doorposts of the house. Where no blood was seen by the Angel of Death, the firstborn in that house would die. However, if the Angel saw blood, he would pass over the house, leaving the firstborn alive. Thus Israel was saved through the sacrifice of a lamb. Later, in the wilderness, God established the sacrificial system with its tabernacle, so that His people's sins could be forgiven based on the death of an animal (Exod. 12:25–27).

All of this helps us to understand the full implications of John the Baptist's announcement upon seeing Jesus: "Behold, the Lamb of God who takes away the sin of the world!" (John 1:29). Jesus is called the "Lamb of God" because He was sent by God to be the ultimate sacrifice for sin, to give His life for sin so that men and women could live. As He hung upon the cross, Jesus took the penalty of our sin upon Himself, thus becoming our sacrifice and our Savior.

His death now brings us life.

Christ is our substitute

Second, Jesus Christ is our substitute: "For Christ also died for sins ... *the just for the unjust.*" Since God is holy, He requires a just sacrifice. Since we are unjust, our sacrifice is unacceptable. So, the perfect Son of God became a man. Being man, He could die in man's place, as our substitute. Being God's sinless Son, He is the *perfect* sacrifice, acceptable to God the Father. Because of this, a wondrous exchange takes place the moment a person turns from his or her sin to trust in Christ for salvation: "He made Him who knew no sin to be sin on our behalf, so that we might become the righteousness of God in Him" (2 Cor. 5:21). As the sinner's substitute, Christ allowed the weight of man's guilt to be placed upon Him on the cross. God the Father then poured out His righteous wrath upon His Son, punishing our sin once and for all (Heb. 7:27). Jesus died *as if* He was guilty, though He was not.

However, there is another side to this exchange. When we as sinners turn to Christ in repentant faith, God credits the righteousness of Christ to our "spiritual bank account" and declares us righteous. We are justified in His sight, not by works, but by faith in the One who took our punishment for us. Galatians 2:16 clearly says, "... knowing that a man is not justified by the works of the Law but through faith in Christ Jesus, even we have believed in Christ Jesus, so that we may be justified by faith in Christ and not by the works of the Law; since by the works of the Law no flesh will be justified." Jesus Christ died to satisfy God's justice and give us life by taking away our sin and gifting us His righteousness.

His death now brings us life.

Christ is our Savior

Third, Jesus Christ is our Savior. "For Christ also died for sins … the just for the unjust, so that He might *bring us to God*." The purpose of God sending His Son was to satisfy His righteousness and justly deal with man's sin. He accomplished this through the sinless life and atoning death of Jesus, which provides the way for the sinner's broken relationship to be restored to what it was at the beginning of time. John says it this way:

> For God so loved the world, that He gave His only begotten Son, that whoever believes in Him shall not perish, but have eternal life. For God did not send the Son into the world to judge the world, but that the world might be saved through Him. He who believes in Him is not judged; he who does not believe has been judged already, because he has not believed in the name of the only begotten Son of God.
>
> John 3:16–18

God has provided salvation through His Son, Jesus Christ. If you will come to Him by faith, you will be forgiven and will receive His gift of eternal life. He who is *the* Savior will become *your* Savior. But all who reject Him stand condemned already and will only see God's face in the final judgment. If [name of deceased] could come back to us today, he/she would reassure us that there is indeed life after death. Death is not the end. For some, it is the beginning of eternity in the presence of God because their trust was in the person and work of Jesus Christ alone. This is how God brings life out of death. For others, it is the beginning of eternity away from God because they refused to repent and instead rejected the One who says, "I am the way, and the truth, and the life; no one comes to the Father but through Me" (John 14:6).

What will death be for you?

72

Why are we here?

... it is appointed for men to die once and after this comes judgment ...

–Hebrews 9:27

It is the experience of death that often causes people to ask questions about life. One of the questions frequently asked is, "Why are we here?" This short life, and this death—it all seems to make no sense. The Lord Jesus Christ answers this question in Matthew 22:34–40.

> But when the Pharisees heard that Jesus had silenced the Sadducees, they gathered themselves together. One of them, a lawyer, asked Him a question, testing Him, "Teacher, which is the great commandment in the Law?" And He said to him, "'You shall love the LORD your God with all your heart, and with all your soul, and with all your mind.' This is the great and foremost commandment. The second is like it, 'You shall love your neighbor as yourself.' On these two commandments depend the whole Law and the Prophets."

Why are we here?

Quite simply, we are here to love God, to love Him with such intensity that it spills over into love for our neighbor. Today, it is often said, "In order to truly love others, you must learn to love yourself." However, Jesus taught something radically different. He taught and lived a life that opposed every shade of self-centeredness, self-esteem, and self-love. He said in effect, "In order to truly love others, you must love God supremely."

However, there is one big glitch in all of this: the Bible teaches that we cannot possibly love God until we have first responded to His love. First John 4:19 says, "We love, because He first loved us." How then do we respond to the love of God? John

3:16 says, "For God so loved the world, that He gave His only begotten Son, that whoever believes in Him shall not perish, but have eternal life."

Why did God send Christ? To meet man's greatest need. Man's greatest need is not world peace, better health care, or to save the environment. Man's greatest need is to be reconciled to God, to have this broken relationship restored. This is what the Scriptures teach.

The need for reconciliation

God's Word tells us that originally man and God enjoyed a very close relationship, but something ruined that. Man chose to violate the direct command of God. Consequently, the relationship was broken. Isaiah 53:6 says, "All of us like sheep have gone astray, each of us has turned to his own way." In Romans 5:12 we read, "Therefore, just as through one man sin entered into the world, and death through sin, and so death spread to all men, because all sinned …" Adam was our representative. When he sinned, we sinned. When he was cast out of God's presence, we were cast out of God's presence; "for all have sinned and fall short of the glory of God" (Rom. 3:23).

Man has an enormous problem. God is holy, but we are sinful. God is righteous, but we are guilty. Being holy, God cannot tolerate sin. So, one party must change. God is God. He will not change. But man, being sinful, cannot become good enough or do enough good things to earn God's favor. Scripture says, "For all of us have become like one who is unclean, and all our righteous deeds are like a filthy garment; and all of us wither like a leaf, and our iniquities, like the wind, take us away" (Isa. 64:6); and "For by grace you have been saved through faith; and that not of yourselves, it is the gift of God; not as a result of works, so that no one may boast" (Eph. 2:8–9). Religion is man reaching out to God. Biblical Christianity is God reaching down to man. If we cannot earn God's favor through church, baptism, charity, confirmation, or any other religious work, how then can we be reconciled to God? God's Word gives the answer.

Just as Adam was our representative through whom we inherited sin, so God provided another representative through whom we may inherit salvation and eternal life. This second Adam is Jesus Christ.

JESUS IS OUR SUBSTITUTE

First Peter 3:18 says, "For Christ also died for sins once for all, the just for the unjust, so that He might bring us to God." Jesus took our place on the cross, enduring the penalty that we earned.

JESUS IS OUR PROPITIATION

"Propitiation" is a big word but one that is too important to ignore. It refers to the satisfaction of the demands of a righteous God, which is what Jesus did on the cross. Romans 3:23–25 says, "… for all have sinned and fall short of the glory of God, being justified as a gift by His grace through the redemption which is in Christ Jesus; whom God displayed publicly as a propitiation in His blood through faith. This was to demonstrate His righteousness." Just as Adam and Eve were cast out of God's presence, so Christ was separated from His Father as a result of our sin. Near the end of three hours of darkness on the cross, during which the Father turned His back on His Son because of our sin, Jesus cried out, "It is finished!" (John 19:30). The purpose for which He was sent to earth was accomplished. He had paid our sin-debt in full.

JESUS IS OUR REDEEMER

To "redeem" means to "buy back." This is what Jesus did when He died. He offered His lifeblood as the purchase price of our redemption. In Ephesians 1:7 we read, "In Him we have redemption through His blood, the forgiveness of our trespasses, according to the riches of His grace." One of the most famous hymns ever written is "The Old Rugged Cross." The third stanza contains these words: "In the old rugged cross, stained with blood so divine, a wondrous beauty I see; for 'twas on that old cross Jesus suffered and died to pardon and sanctify me."[1]

God Himself has provided the way to be reconciled to Him. However, that does not mean that we are automatically forgiven. God's Word insists that this demonstration of God's love must be applied personally by faith. John 3:36 makes it clear that "He who believes in the Son has eternal life; but he who does not obey the Son will not see life, but the wrath of God abides on him." But this is difficult for us to accept. Our nature wants us to earn everything we receive. So God must bring us to the end of ourselves. We must see how helpless we really are. Funerals remind us of the fact that we are dependent on God for our every breath, whether we acknowledge that truth or not.

When you die and stand before your holy Creator, there will only be one issue. It is not which church you belonged to, or whether or not you were baptized by your parents or confirmed by your church, or whether you gave money to charity. The one issue will be: "What did you do with Jesus Christ?" So how will you respond to God's love as demonstrated by His Son Jesus Christ?

In Psalm 39:4 we read, "LORD, make me to know my end and what is the extent of my days; let me know how transient I am." These words remind us that life on this earth is temporary and unsure. It has been said that everything in life is uncertain except death. James, the brother of Jesus, reminds us of this when he writes, "Yet you do not know what your life will be like tomorrow. You are just a vapor that appears for a little while and then vanishes away" (James 4:14).

At times like these, when life's activities seem to come to a sudden halt, God would be pleased for us to pause and examine the state of our own souls. This solemn occasion reminds us of the uncertainty of life. Any of us may be called next. The question we must all ask ourselves is, "Am I prepared?" Peter

Marshall, a Scottish-American preacher and Chaplain of the US Senate in the first half of the twentieth century, once told the following story:

> An old legend tells of a merchant in Baghdad who one day sent his servants to the market. Before very long the servant came back, white and trembling, and in great agitation said to this master: "Down in the market place I was jostled by a woman in the crowd, and when I turned around I saw it was Death that jostled me. She looked at me and made a threatening gesture. Master, please lend me your horse, for I must hasten away to avoid her. I will ride to Samara and there I will hide, and Death will not find me."
>
> The merchant lent him his horse and the servant galloped away in great haste. Later the merchant went down to the market place and saw Death standing in the crowd. He went over to her and asked, "Why did you frighten my servant this morning? Why did you make a threatening gesture?"
>
> "That was not a threatening gesture," Death said. "It was only a start of surprise. I was astonished to see him in Baghdad, for I have an appointment with him tonight in Samara."
>
> Each of us has an appointment in Samara. But that is cause for rejoicing—not for fear, provided we have put our trust in Him who alone holds the keys to life and death.[2]

Each of us has an appointment with God. Scripture says, "… it is appointed for men to die once and after this comes judgment" (Heb. 9:27). Because none of us knows the day that has been appointed for us to die, the time to examine our own hearts is today. The Holy Spirit is saying to us, "Today if you hear His voice, do not harden your hearts" (Heb. 3:7–8). Every time we ignore or turn away from the truth of God's Word, we are hardening our hearts. Today, God is graciously warning us that to do so is to take one more step toward our hearts being hardened forever. This is not what God wants for us. He has graciously given His Son, the Lord Jesus Christ, as His gift. I exhort you to come to God through Him. Jesus says, "I am the way, and the truth, and the life; no one comes to the Father but through Me" (John 14:6). There is no other way to God; "how will we escape if we neglect so great a salvation?" (Heb. 2:3).

The reality of death and eternal life[I]

In loving memory of Jean C. Pitz
June 9, 1953–April 12, 2008

Chapter 7

No guilt in life, no fear in death—
This is the pow'r of Christ in me;
From life's first cry to final breath,
Jesus commands my destiny.
No pow'r of hell, no scheme of man,
Can ever pluck me from His hand;
Till He returns or calls me home—
Here in the pow'r of Christ I'll stand.

–Keith Getty and Stuart Townend[2]

One of the commonest statements we hear when someone has died is this: "Well, at least he or she is in a better place. At least he or she is not in pain anymore." But are people really sure of this? Or do they say it in order to ease their own pain or to fight off the doubts they really feel deep down in their hearts? How do we even know there is "a better place"? And how can we know how to get there if such a place does exist? How can we know what will happen when we die? How do we know that eternal life in heaven is not just something that man made up just to feel better about death? These are the kinds of questions people ask. And these are the kinds of issues that funerals force us to think about—if we will stop long enough to think.

Jesus Christ the Son of God said more about heaven and hell than anyone else has done. It is His words that we must listen to today. Specifically, I want us to open our ears to one brief statement. Jesus says, "Truly, truly, I say to you, he who hears My word, and believes Him who sent Me, has eternal life, and does not come into judgment, but has passed out of death into life" (John 5:24).

There are three basic truths in this verse.

Eternal judgment is a reality

There is a literal place called hell and people really do go there. Revelation 20:11–15 says,

> Then I saw a great white throne and Him who sat upon it, from whose presence earth and heaven fled away, and no place was found for them. And I saw the dead, the great and the small, standing before the throne, and books were opened; and another book was opened, which is the book of life; and the dead were judged from the things which were written in the books, according to their deeds. And the sea gave up the dead which were in it, and death and Hades gave up the dead which were in them; and they were judged, every one of them according to their deeds. Then death and Hades were thrown into the lake of fire. This is the second death, the lake of fire. And if anyone's name was not found written in the book of life, he was thrown into the lake of fire.

Eternal life is a reality

There is a literal place called heaven and people really do go there. Revelation 21:23–27 says,

> And the city has no need of the sun or of the moon to shine on it, for the glory of God has illumined it, and its lamp is the Lamb. The nations will walk by its light, and the kings of the earth will bring their glory into it. In the daytime (for there will be no night there) its gates will never be closed; and they will bring the glory and the honor of the nations into it; and nothing unclean, and no one who practices abomination and lying, shall ever come into it, but only those whose names are written in the Lamb's book of life.

You must choose between God's judgment and His offer of eternal life

Every person will spend eternity somewhere. Heaven and hell are the only two eternal homes. You must choose between the two. Hebrews 9:27–28 says, "And inasmuch as it is appointed for men to die once and after this comes judgment, so Christ also, having been offered once to bear the sins of many, will appear a second time for salvation without reference to sin, to those who eagerly await Him."

Jesus says, "Truly, truly, I say to you, he who hears My word, and believes Him who sent Me, has eternal life, and does not come into judgment, but has passed out of death into life" (John 5:24).

This is the message that Jean wants you to hear. If there is one thing that she wants you to understand today it is this: Jean Pitz is a sinner saved by grace. Jean Pitz was not saved by God because she was special. She was special because she was saved by God.

Over the past two days, I have looked at every page in Jean's personal Bible. I have read every handwritten word, comment, and sermon note. I have touched every dog-eared page. The margins of her Bible are filled with explanatory comments she heard in sermons, her own outlines, and simple drawings. I want to share some of her notes with you because they reveal how personal Jean's walk with God really was. As I read over her comments, they naturally fell into four groups, which reveal certain characteristics of Jean.

She was a student of the Word

- Psalm 19: "When life is bitter, God's Word is like honey."
- 1 John 3: "No believer is who he or she should be, but we will be when we see Christ."

In the thirty years that Jean was a Christian, she never lost her simple appreciation for what Christ had done for her and, therefore, she was always hungry to learn more from His Word.

She actively trusted in God in the face of trouble

- Psalm 4: "Peace, joy, and security are found in Him alone—not in our circumstances."
- Psalm 6: "Pray and let God handle it—don't avenge evil."
- Psalm 86: "God is trustworthy. Learn to hang on to Him, no matter what you are going through."

She never forgot her salvation

Over the sixteen years that I knew Jean, I noticed that she never thought of herself as better than others. The reason for this is that she never lost sight of the kind of life that Christ had saved her from. She knew that she was still a sinner fighting to live for God but saved by His amazing grace. Twice she wrote in her Bible that her favorite verse was 1 Corinthians 10:13, which says, "No temptation has overtaken you but such as is common to man; and God is faithful, who will not allow you to be tempted beyond what you are able, but with the temptation will provide the way of escape also, so that you will be able to endure it." Jean knew that, even though she was saved and forgiven, she would always face temptation to sin. But she also knew that the God who had saved her would give her a way of escape. Now she is free; she has escaped from sin—forever.

She tried to live in the light of eternity

- Ecclesiastes: "Who will remember me in 100 years?" This revealed her desire to live for God now, while she had the chance.
- Ecclesiastes: "The question at the end of life is, have we feared God and obeyed God?"

- Isaiah: "You can do all the right things in all the right ways, but if your heart is full of sin, you are not worshiping God."

On the very last page of her Bible, Jean wrote these words in red ink: "After we have served God's purpose, we will die."

Jean did not fear death because she had already received eternal life. She trusted what Jesus says: "Truly, truly, I say to you, he who hears My word, and believes Him who sent Me, has eternal life, and does not come into judgment, but has passed out of death into life" (John 5:24).

Jean was like an older sister to me, and I think that there is one thing I will remember the most about her: she always had a word of encouragement. Specifically, there was one message she continually said to me. "Paul," she would often say after a morning church service, "don't ever stop telling us that we must repent of our sins and come to Jesus. I grew up in this church and heard it over and over again and yet I did not turn from my sinful ways until I was in my twenties. Don't ever assume that everyone in this church truly believes. Keep preaching the gospel."

Jean was always concerned about the next generation of young people who would grow up in this church. She was concerned that they hear the message that Jesus saves. She did not want them to wander from God as she did. She wanted them to come to Christ early in life and be saved. To the boys and girls and young people here today, Mrs. Pitz would say this: "Repent and come to Jesus today. Sin will deceive you, but Jesus will never disappoint you."

My friends, there is an eternally important reason why you are here today. God chose to end Jean's earthly life earlier than we expected because His purpose, which we may never fully understand, had been fulfilled in her. However, another reason why He took her home was so that you would be here today to hear the good news that Jesus Christ came into the world to save sinners like you and me.

If Jean were here today, she would say, "Come to Jesus. Leave your life of sin. Come to Jesus and receive God's free gift of salvation. Be forgiven. He will take your guilt away. Stop running from Him. Stop trying to make yourself better. Stop trying to ease your pain by filling your life with more and more things. Come to Jesus, and He will give you a new life. He is the only source of true joy in this world. Come to Christ today. Do not wait until tomorrow."

Jesus says to us, "Truly, truly, I say to you, he who hears My word, and believes Him who sent Me, has eternal life, and does not come into judgment, but has passed out of death into life" (John 5:24).

At this very moment, you stand at a fork in the road of your life, and the path you choose will determine your eternal destiny. You must choose to go one of two ways: either remain in your sin and unbelief, or turn away from sin to God. Today can be the first day of a totally new life in Christ. Turn to Him now. In your heart, agree with God that you are a sinner in desperate need of His mercy and grace. Call upon Jesus. Be saved today before it is eternally too late.

On the death of an infant[I]

In loving memory of Seth Isaiah Freel
October 5, 1999–October 5, 1999

Chapter 8

Small coffins are placed in the ground, but more than the body is buried.

–James W. Bruce, III[2]

In Deuteronomy 29:29, we read these words: "The secret things belong to the LORD our God, but the things revealed belong to us and to our sons forever, that we may observe all the words of this law." This verse teaches us three great truths about God.

Truth 1. God keeps some things secret

The secret things that belong only to God include the divine purposes behind His divine decrees. We seldom understand God's ways because He who created the universe is infinite.

> Remember the former things long past,
>   For I am God, and there is no other;
>   I am God, and there is no one like Me,
> Declaring the end from the beginning,
>   And from ancient times things which have not been done,
>   Saying, "My purpose will be established,
>   And I will accomplish all My good pleasure."
>
> Isa. 46:9–10

> Oh, the depth of the riches both of the wisdom
> and knowledge of God! How unsearchable are
> His judgments and unfathomable His ways!
>
> Rom. 11:33

> Great is the LORD, and highly to be praised,
>   And His greatness is unsearchable.
>
> Ps. 145:3

> "For My thoughts are not your thoughts,
>   Nor are your ways My ways," declares the LORD.
> For as the heavens are higher than the earth,

> So are My ways higher than your ways
> And My thoughts than your thoughts.
>
> Isa. 55:8–9

It is clear that God's thoughts and purposes are infinitely above our own. In our limited human minds, we do not understand why God created Seth and then chose to end his life before we could have the joy of knowing him. But that is OK. God doesn't call us to live in the realm of the secret things. He calls us to rest in His unchanging nature and character. He is the Sovereign One. He calls us to stand upon Him, for He is our Rock and our Fortress (Ps. 46).

There is a second truth before us.

Truth 2. God has revealed what it is necessary for us to know

Deuteronomy 29:29 goes on, "but the things revealed belong to us and to our sons forever." Although there are some things we will never know, there is a great deal that we do know. Let us set aside what we cannot understand and focus on what God has revealed in His Word concerning all that we need to know. For example:

WE KNOW THAT GOD IS GOOD

> Good and upright is the LORD;
>   therefore He instructs sinners in the way.
>
> Ps. 25:8

James, the brother of Jesus, writes, "Every good thing given and every perfect gift is from above, coming down from the Father of lights, with whom there is no variation or shifting shadow" (James 1:17).

WE KNOW THAT GOD IS HOLY

> Exalt the LORD our God

And worship at His holy hill,
For holy is the LORD our God.

Ps. 99:9

Being holy, He is totally distinct from all of His creatures. God is completely without sin or defilement of any kind.

WE KNOW THAT GOD IS RIGHTEOUS AND KIND

The LORD is righteous in all His ways
And kind in all His deeds.

Ps. 145:17

God always does what He knows is right. He never makes mistakes. Whether or not we fully understand His ways is not important. What is important is that by faith we know that God is righteous and kind, and we cling to this truth.

WE KNOW THAT GOD GIVES AND GOD TAKES AWAY

Then Job arose and tore his robe and shaved his head,
and he fell to the ground and worshiped. He said,
 "Naked I came from my mother's womb,
 And naked I shall return there.
 The LORD gave and the LORD has taken away.
 Blessed be the name of the LORD."
Through all this Job did not sin nor did he blame God.

Job 1:20–22

WE KNOW THAT GOD CREATED MAN FOR HIS GLORY

Everyone who is called by My name,
 And whom I have created for My glory,
 Whom I have formed, even whom I have made.

Isa. 43:7

God created man in order to pour out His love upon him, and when man finds complete joy and satisfaction in his Creator, God is glorified. Having created Adam and Eve in His image, the triune Godhead enjoyed fellowship with man.

WE KNOW THAT MAN REBELLED AGAINST GOD'S GOOD COMMAND AND BROUGHT A CURSE UPON HIMSELF ACCORDING TO GENESIS 3

In the beginning, God created man from the dust of the earth and breathed into him the breath of life. As creatures made in the image of God, man and woman enjoyed a unique relationship with their Creator God. God told them that this intimate fellowship would continue as long as they remained obedient to His command not to eat from the tree of the knowledge of good and evil. If they disobeyed, they would surely die. Man and woman chose to rebel against the clear command of God. Death came as a result. Spiritual death came: immediately they knew that they were no longer at peace with God. Physical death also came: God killed an animal and made clothing out of the skins. This was the first sign that God would accept a sacrifice for sin. At a later date, Adam and Eve's own physical lives also came to an end (Gen. 5:5).

WE KNOW THAT GOD ALLOWED SINFUL MAN TO HAVE A RELATIONSHIP WITH HIM ON THE BASIS OF A SACRIFICE

About two thousand years after Adam, God commanded a man named Abraham to offer his son as a sacrifice in order to test his love. Abraham obeyed, but before his son Isaac's life was taken, God provided a ram to be offered in place of Isaac (Gen. 22).

During the time of Moses, God delivered His people from Egyptian bondage. Before the tenth plague was brought upon the nation, God instructed His people that each household should kill a lamb and sprinkle its blood on the doorposts of the house. Where no blood was seen by the Angel of Death, the firstborn in that house would die. However, if the Angel saw blood, he would pass over the house, leaving the firstborn alive. Thus Israel was saved through a sacrifice (Exod. 12).

Later, in the wilderness, God commanded Moses to build the tabernacle, where sacrifices were offered so that the sins of the people could be forgiven (Exod. 25–27). All of this helps us to understand the full implication of John the Baptist's announcement as he saw Jesus walking toward him: "Behold, the Lamb of God who takes away the sin of the world" (John 1:29).

WE KNOW THAT THE SON OF GOD BECAME MAN IN ORDER TO FULFILL GOD'S PROMISE TO PROVIDE THE ULTIMATE SACRIFICE—A REDEEMER

Jesus was called "the Lamb of God" because He was sent by God to be the perfect sacrifice for sin, to die so that men and women could live. As He hung upon the cross, Jesus took the penalty of our sin upon Himself, thus becoming our sacrifice. His death now brings us life. First Peter 3:18 reads, "For Christ also died for sins once for all, the just for the unjust, so that He might bring us to God, having been put to death in the flesh, but made alive in the spirit."

Since God is holy, He requires a just sacrifice. Since we are unjust, our sacrifice is unacceptable. So the perfect Son of God became a man. Being man, He could die in man's place, as his substitute. And, being God, He could die as the perfect sacrifice, acceptable to God.

Because of this truth, a wondrous exchange takes place the moment a person turns from his or her sin to trust in Christ for salvation. Second Corinthians 5:21 says, "He made Him who knew no sin to be sin on our behalf, so that we might become the righteousness of God in Him." As the sinner's substitute, Christ allowed the weight of our guilt to be placed upon Him on the cross. God the Father then poured out His righteous wrath upon His Son, punishing sin once and for all (Heb. 10:10).

When we as sinners turn to God in repentance, trusting in the sacrifice of Christ on our behalf, God forgives our sin and credits the righteousness of Christ to us, and we are justified. As our substitute, Christ died to satisfy God's justice and to demonstrate His love. Romans 5:6–8 says, "For while we were still helpless, at the right time Christ died for the ungodly. For one will hardly die for a righteous man; though perhaps for the good man someone would dare even to die. But God

95

demonstrates His own love toward us, in that while we were yet sinners, Christ died for us."

WE KNOW THAT THE RESURRECTION OF JESUS CHRIST GUARANTEES ETERNAL LIFE FOR ALL WHO TRUST IN HIM FOR THEIR SALVATION

Death is often viewed as the end, but it is not. The main message of the Bible is that the death, burial, and resurrection of Christ bring hope to sinners. Romans 6:23 says, "For the wages of sin is death, but the free gift of God is eternal life in Christ Jesus our Lord." While grieving the death of his infant son, King David said, "But now he has died; why should I fast? Can I bring him back again? I will go to him, but he will not return to me" (2 Sam. 12:23). Seth's parents possess this same confidence and hope because their trust is in Jesus Christ as Lord and Savior. Knowing Christ means that they have an eternal home in heaven. It also means that they will see Seth again.

Our verse contains a third truth.

Truth 3. God holds us accountable for how we respond to His revealed truth

Deuteronomy 29:29 says, "The secret things belong to the LORD our God, but the things revealed belong to us and to our sons forever"; however, the verse concludes with these words: "that we may observe all the words of this law." God doesn't call us to understand the secret things that belong to Him; He only expects us to respond to the truth that He has revealed to us in the Scriptures.

My friends, you have been summoned here today by God. It is no accident that Seth's short life has ended. It is no accident that you are sitting here tonight listening to the Word of God. My question to you is not, "Do you understand why God has chosen to do what He has done?" but rather, "How will you respond to the spiritual truth God has revealed to you in His Word?"

God has provided salvation through His Son, Jesus Christ.

All who will come to Him in repentant faith are forgiven, stand justified before their holy Creator, and will one day spend eternity in His presence. All who reject Him already stand condemned and will only see God's face in the final judgment.

When something happens that we do not understand, we have a choice to make. We can demand to know the secret things, doubt God, and possibly even become angry and bitter against Him; or we can surrender our limited understanding and trust God. We do not know everything, but we do know that we have a God who can be trusted to make no mistakes. He is holy and righteous and good, and in this we rejoice.

> God never moves without purpose or plan,
> When trying His servant and molding a man.
> Give thanks to the Lord though your testing seems long;
> In darkness He giveth a song.
>
> *O rejoice in the Lord! He makes no mistake.*
> *He knoweth the end of each path that I take.*
> *For when I am tried and purified, I shall come forth as gold.*
>
> I could not see through the shadows ahead;
> So I looked at the cross of my Savior instead.
> I bowed to the will of the Master that day;
> Then peace came and tears fled away.
>
> Now I can see testing comes from above;
> God strengthens His children and purges in love.
> My Father knows best, and I trust in His care;
> Through purging more fruit I will bear.[3]

Part 3:
Practical helps
for fellow
comforters

I n *Suffering and the Sovereignty of God*, Dustin Shramek provides this plain counsel: "We love them by first weeping with them."[1] This simple description of comforting those who grieve is consistent with the biblical admonition to "Rejoice with those who rejoice, and weep with those who weep" (Rom. 12:15). The familial bonds in the church, the family of God, demand that we care for one another in times of grief and pain. We should imagine nothing less. Deborah Howard asks,

> What can we do to help those experiencing grief?
> First we must be where we can see the problem—in
> contact with those we suspect are hurting. One
> of the most important things we can do is just to
> be there. Our presence speaks louder than words.
> There are two things we need to take them every
> time we go—hope and a tender, listening heart. We
> don't have to come up with flowery phrases. Sitting
> quietly with them is more comforting than preaching
> sermons to them. And sometimes we can gently direct
> their thinking toward the faithfulness of God.[2]

This section contains nothing profound. Rather, it simply reflects my own attempt "to be there" for the grieving members of my flock. I have made my share of mistakes as a pastor, but God is gracious in continuing to help me grow to be more faithful as an undershepherd of His flock. The following are some practical helps that may also encourage your growth as a fellow minister of the gospel.

Chapter 9 is a call for extended ministry to the bereaved, including a suggested plan for sixteen months of follow-up care that activates members of the body of Christ to serve one another with compassion. The biblical analogy between the church and the human body has numerous implications for grief ministry. Since when "one member suffers, all the members suffer with it"

(1 Cor. 12:26), no one in the church should have to walk through the valley of the shadow of death alone—ever!

Chapter 10 is a plea to ministers of the gospel to consider getting involved in hospice care by making themselves available to serve as volunteer chaplains and/or equipping members of their flocks to make spiritually impacting visits. Included are teaching outlines that will mobilize a small team of men and women in your church to minister grace at the bedsides of those who are dying.

Appendix 1 contains two simple lists of Scriptures that might be helpful when comforting others. When I served as a hospice chaplain, I distributed countless copies of laminated cards with these texts to servants in my church and to the family members of those approaching death.

Since I envision that some may bring this small book with them on visits to the sick, dying, and bereaved, Appendix 2 is a collection of poetry, hymns, and prayers that are sure to bring comfort to the sorrowful when read out loud by a compassionate caregiver. The biblical book of Psalms is the one and only divinely inspired book of poetry, songs, and prayers and should, therefore, be top priority. However, the words of other saints throughout church history may surely be used to bring comfort as well, provided that they are consistent with biblical theology.

Appendix 3 consists of four sample memorial services that will be of help to the minister who serves as officiant. Care and sensitivity, without compromising the integrity of the gospel message, should be taken in the planning of these services. Whether the deceased is a believer or an unbeliever, the officiant must always hold forth the good news of Jesus Christ as the only hope for sinners. Remember: gospel-centered comfort is the only true comfort.

Finally, Appendix 4 gives a list of helpful resources that every minister of God's grace should consider making part of his library. The numerous books listed will encourage personal growth as a pastor, while other resources serve as excellent tools of outreach to the bereaved.

After the funeral

Chapter 9

We are God's loved ones, the Bride of Christ our Lord,
For we have known it, the love of God outpoured;
Now let us learn how to return the gift of love once
  given:
O let us share each joy and care,
And live with a zeal that pleases Heaven.

–Bryan Jeffrey Leech[1]

"The pastor saw me right after my husband's death, and he met with me before the service. He said a few words at the funeral. But I never saw him again in regard to my husband's death. My real struggles didn't begin until two weeks after the funeral, and by then, everyone was out of sight."[2] Sadly, this is too often true. Kevin Ruffcorn therefore comments, "The memorial service is not the place to terminate ministry to the bereaved. It is the place to begin a different but no less important one."[3] Ministering to those who have lost a loved one is a unique privilege and responsibility.

Support for those experiencing loss needs to extend far beyond the traditional sympathy card to phone calls, visits, and Christian fellowship over meals. We must intentionally help those who grieve to adjust to the reality of the changes that have shaken their world.

It is impossible to overemphasize the importance of getting members of the church family involved in comforting one another. The bereaved also need to be encouraged to "stay connected." Paul Tripp admonishes the grieving person, "God likens the church to a physical body of interconnected and interdependent parts. He reminds us that life is a community project. In grief, it is tempting to turn inside yourself and avoid the community around you."[4] Therefore, pastors must gently urge those who are grieving to resist the temptation to "pull away" and instead remain as involved as possible in the normal body life of the church.

Sixteen-month bereavement care

When serving as a volunteer chaplain for a local hospice, I was impressed by how long the nursing staff followed up the family of the deceased. It made me wonder why I as a pastor did not do something like that for the people in my church. Since that time, I have sought to be more intentional as a shepherd in continuing to care for the bereaved long after the memorial service is over, the flowers have wilted, the phone stops ringing, and the mailman no longer delivers cards or letters. The following chart is merely an example of a plan that was designed to comfort and encourage a widower in my church and his extended family. Every minister of God's grace should come up with his own plan, which will vary from person to person and change along the way, but will prevent the bereaved from being forgotten by the church family or from slipping through the cracks of a busy ministry. Notice how the care begins on a weekly basis, primarily from a pastor, and gradually transitions to monthly care provided by others in the church, but still under the oversight of a church shepherd.

Week following the death	Personal contact	Primary caregiver	Done
Week 1	Take widower to lunch. Send sympathy cards to all relatives in the church. Include copies of comforting hymn lyrics inside the cards you send. Give the widower an appropriate sermon CD, such as "God's Delight in the Death of a Believer."	Pastor	
Week 2	Phone call Written copies of funeral sermon to all family members if deemed appropriate.	Pastor	
Week 3	Lunch	Pastor	

Week 4	Send "Praying for you" cards to family members. Try to remember key holidays that will be especially difficult the first year following the death, such as the birthday of the deceased, Mother's Day, wedding anniversary, etc. Put reminders on your computer/in your diary.	Pastor	
Week 5	Lunch	Man in church	
Week 6	Give widower a small booklet to read, such as *Heaven* by Jonathan Edwards. [If the bereaved person is ready for a larger book, I highly recommend *Sunsets: Reflections for Life's Final Journey* by hospice nurse Deborah Howard. If the deceased was a child, I highly recommend *From Grief to Glory* by James Bruce (resources listed in Appendix 4).]	Pastor	
Week 7	Phone call	Deacon	
Week 8	Send a list of comforting Scriptures	Pastor	
Week 10	Lunch	Deacon and others	
Week 12	Give him a small booklet, such as *Grief: Finding Hope Again* by Paul David Tripp [also listed in Appendix 4].	Pastor	
Week 14	Phone call	Man in church	
Week 16	Invite him to your house for a light snack after Sunday evening service, with a few others from church.	Pastor, deacon, or ask another family in church	
Month 5	Have some form of personal contact at least once a month. Be creative.	Involve as many others in the church family as possible.	
Month 6			
Month 7			
Month 8			
Month 9			
Month 10			
Month 11			
ONE YEAR: anniversary of the death	[This will be a hard day for most people. They will need some form of personal contact: a hand to hold, a hug, some type of physical contact. They need reassurance of how God has faithfully brought them through the past year.]	Pastor should ask a friend of the bereaved to provide this encouragement.	

Month 13	Have some form of personal contact at least once a month. Be creative.	Involve as many others in the church family as possible.	
Month 14			
Month 15			
Month 16	Lunch	Pastor and a deacon	

When the primary griever is a woman, the minister who is married should bring his wife along when making visits. The unmarried pastor should bring along a few other church members (ideally a mature couple) in order to avoid sending an improper message or putting any temptation before the bereaved or himself. This will also immediately give the grieving woman another "contact" in the church to reach out to when needed. In keeping with the Titus 2:3–5 philosophy of ministry, church shepherds, married and unmarried alike, should get other spiritually mature women in the church involved as soon as possible and transition the personal care to them while remaining available to provide counsel to the primary caregivers. Teaching shepherds should always equip their sheep to care for one another in the flock, which is the main subject of my book *Counsel Your Flock*.[5] The experience of grief in a local church becomes a time to test how effectively believers have been, and are being, prepared to serve one another. The faithful pastor who diligently equips his church members for ministry will be pleasantly surprised, and deeply fulfilled, by the initiative they show in times of loss.

In the particular case of this widower, much more one-another ministry was carried out spontaneously by other members of the church body. For example, I heard of numerous families who invited the bereaved families over for a meal, as well as men who took the new widower out to lunch. The pastor will do his flock much good by constantly teaching other-member care and the practice of biblical fellowship in the church. It is a delight to watch a well-trained body function as God designed.

Serving as a hospice chaplain

Then the righteous will answer Him, "Lord, when did we see You hungry, and feed You, or thirsty, and give You something to drink? And when did we see You a stranger, and invite You in, or naked, and clothe You? When did we see You sick, or in prison, and come to You?" The King will answer and say to them, "Truly I say to you, to the extent that you did it to one of these brothers of Mine, even the least of them, you did it to Me."

–Matthew 25:37–40

The compassion of Jesus is most often demonstrated in small ways. It is the drink of water to the one dying of thirst or the visit to the stranger in need of the company of a friend that the King of Heaven will one day reward. Therefore, as a minister of God's grace and comfort, please consider contacting one of your local hospice organizations to offer your assistance as a volunteer chaplain. During the three years that I served in this way, I was startled to realize how many people went through the experience of death without any spiritual support. This pattern continues to be prevalent in our non-personal society. Many times it is because the dying person has not been faithful to a local church of any kind. Other times, pastors avoid this difficult part of church ministry because they feel ill-prepared or fear that the person may not be receptive. Whatever the cause of this vacuum, it must be filled, and it is best if it gets filled by those committed to the biblical gospel. Pray about whether or not God may use you to fill this need in your local area. You will be surprised at the doors that may open for the gospel.

After you gain some experience ministering to the dying, consider training a team of men and women in your church to minister in an unofficial capacity as volunteer caregivers.[1] The following are teaching outlines that I used when preparing a team like this in my church.

The first visit: establishing rapport by showing compassion

The goal of your first visit is threefold:

- To establish a rapport (sympathetic relationship) with the dying person and his or her family.
- To offer genuine help and comfort.
- To meet any urgent spiritual needs that may either be expressed by the person who is dying or by his or her family members, or be discerned by you.

The following five-step process will enable you to meet the stated goal of your first visit. Unless the family desires your continued presence, you should try to keep your visits to around fifteen minutes (thirty at the most).

1. ESTABLISH UNDERSTANDING: "BE QUICK TO HEAR, SLOW TO SPEAK" (JAMES 1:19)

- Offer a tender touch.
- Ask questions. This shows that you care and that you have not come with your own agenda; the person in need sets your agenda.
- Listen to the heart in order to hear what is behind the person's words (fear, worry, doubt, etc.). Ask the Holy Spirit to make you sensitive.
- Discern any immediate needs or fears.

2. SHOW COMPASSION

- Empathize with the person's pain.
- Calm the person's fears with tender words of promise from God. In the case of an unbeliever, assure him or her that God cares for His creation and that He desires to make Himself known to that person in this time of suffering.

- Be sensitive to immediate needs.
- Always speak graciously.

3. OBTAIN PERMISSION

Don't barge into the person's life like a bombastic preacher. Instead, gently ask questions such as:

- Do you have any favorite Scripture passages that I may read to you?
- Do you have any spiritual needs that I can help you with?
- May I pray for you?

If the dying person is unable to communicate and a spouse, parent, or other family member is present, ask that family member the above questions. The key is that you want the person to "invite you into his or her life." This breaks down any walls that may hinder your ministry from being received.

4. DISPENSE BIBLICAL COMFORT AND HOPE

- Be committed to truth in spirituality. The Word of God is truth (John 8:32; 17:17).
- Remind the sufferer that God is the "God of all comfort" (2 Cor. 1:3).
- Read appropriate Scriptures and offer to pray with the person.

5. GIVE THE PERSON ASSURANCE OF YOUR CONTINUED PRAYERS AND SUPPORT

Future visits: addressing specific spiritual needs

Assuming you have established a rapport with the dying person and sense receptiveness to your ministry, you can now begin to address specific spiritual needs. Unless the person you are ministering to has clearly communicated his or her present spiritual condition, you cannot assume too much. Therefore, you must begin with basic biblical truths. Regardless of their religious background, most dying people have a basic respect for the Bible and will permit you to read it to them. The goal is to get beyond religion to a simple, childlike trust in the finished work of Jesus Christ on the cross of Calvary. This is the only source of true hope for the dying.

The following is a brief summary of how to graciously communicate the hope of the gospel. On the assumption that the patient's attention span will be short, due to medication and declining health, the Scripture portions are brief. If attention span is not an issue, longer passages may be used (see Appendix 1). Before reading Scripture, remind the patient that the words he or she is hearing are God's words, not your words. Silently pray for the Spirit to give the patient understanding as you read.

COMMUNICATE THE HOPE OF THE GOSPEL OF JESUS CHRIST

Example 1: How to find peace with God
- How sin broke man's fellowship with his holy Creator: Genesis 2:15–17; 3:17–24.
- How God took the initiative to restore fellowship: John 3:16–18; Romans 5:6–8.
- What man must do to be restored to peace with God: Romans 5:1; 10:9–10.

Example 2: How to find forgiveness of sin
- Why man needs to be forgiven—"The bad news": Habakkuk 1:13; Isaiah 53:6; Romans 3:23; Hebrews 9:27.
- Why forgiveness is available—"The good news": Romans 5:8; 6:23; John 19:30 with Colossians 2:14.
- How to be forgiven: John 5:24; Acts 17:30–31.

Unless we communicate the bad news, the good news loses all its meaning. The bad news is that sin separates man from God, but the good news is that God sent His only begotten Son to pay the penalty for man's sin in order to reconcile sinners back to God.

COMPEL THE PERSON TO GO BEYOND RELIGION TO FAITH IN CHRIST ALONE

Religion gives man no hope because there is always one more good deed that can be done or one more religious rite to be performed. Hope is found only in believing that when Christ said on the cross, "It is finished!" (John 19:30), He meant it. The debt of sin has already been paid. As a result, God offers the gift of eternal life to those who repent and believe the gospel. Use Ephesians 2:8–9 and 1 John 5:11–13 to call the sufferer to faith in Jesus.

Offer to pray for and with the person, asking God to grant him or her the twin gifts of faith and repentance that he or she might flee *from* unbelief *to* Christ for salvation.

Witnessing cards

Print the following cards double-sided and laminate them. Keep them in your wallet for your own use and give them to those you train as hospice caregivers.

Giving spiritual hope to the dying

How to find peace with God

Assuming you have gained permission from the patient or his/her family, read:

- How sin broke man's relationship with God: Gen. 2:15–17; 3:17–24.
- How God took the initiative to restore the relationship: John 3:16–18; Rom. 5:6–8.
- What man must do to be restored to peace with God: Rom. 5:1; 10:9–10.

Giving spiritual hope to the dying

How to find forgiveness of sin

Assuming you have gained permission from the patient or his/her family, read:

- Why man needs to be forgiven—"The bad news": Isa. 53:6; Rom. 3:23; Heb. 9:27.
- Why forgiveness is available—"The good news": Rom. 5:8; 6:23; John 19:30 with Col. 2:14.
- How to be forgiven: John 5:24; Acts 17:30–31.

General principles for grief care

To effectively minister God's grace in times of loss, we must remind ourselves of the comforting character and ministry of God. During the process of grieving, the people who are experiencing loss need a great deal of reassurance.

REMIND YOURSELF OF BIBLICAL PRINCIPLES FOR GRIEF AFTERCARE

Remind yourself of biblical examples of grieving
- Abraham grieved the loss of his wife, Sarah, in Genesis 23:2. Here the Hebrew word "mourn" (*caphad*) means to tear the heart and beat the breast. The Hebrew word "weep" (*bakah*) means to lament with great sorrow.
- Mary, Martha, and Jesus grieved the loss of Lazarus (John 11).

Remind yourself of the power of the Word of God to meet man's deepest needs (Ps. 19:7–11)

REASSURE THOSE EXPERIENCING LOSS
- Reassure them that grieving is not sin: "Blessed are those

who mourn" (Matt. 5:4). Refer to biblical examples of those who grieved, including Jesus (noted above).

- Reassure them of the character and comfort of God: "God is our refuge and strength, a very present help in trouble" (Ps. 46:1). Other texts include 2 Corinthians 1:3 and Psalm 111.
- Reassure them through the ministry of your presence and prayers (Col. 3:12; James 5:16).
- Reassure them of the need to let others serve them (Phil. 2:3–4).
- Reassure them that God will walk through the future *with* them (Ps. 23 with John 10:11–15).

REAFFIRM YOUR COMMITMENT TO THEM

"A friend loves at all times" (Prov. 17:17).

Scriptures
that comfort

Print the following lists double-sided and laminate them. Keep them in your wallet for your own use and keep a supply on hand to give to family and friends ministering to their loved ones.

Food for the soul

When in need of strength—Psalm 46
When in fear—Psalm 23
When discouraged—Isaiah 40
When filled with anxiety—Matthew 6:19–34
When bitterness has set in—1 Corinthians 13:1–7
When life seems bigger than God—Psalm 90
When God seems distant—Psalm 139
When in need of peace and rest—Matthew 11:25–30
The secret of happiness—Matthew 5:1–9
For a description of heaven—Revelation 21

Food for the soul

When in need of mercy—Psalm 103
When concerned about forgiveness—Psalm 51:1–13
When concerned about eternal life—John 3:1–21
Who is Jesus Christ?—John 20:30–31; 1 John 5:11–13
Why did Jesus come?—Isaiah 53; Romans 5
God's plan of salvation—Ephesians 2:1–10
Christ, Mediator for man—1 Timothy 2:5–6
When concerned about faith—Hebrews 11
God's unfailing love—Romans 8:31–39
The goodness of God—Psalm 111

Poetry, songs, and prayers for comfort

The unsearchable ways of God

In memory of Rachel M. Matt
By Paul Tautges

Sometimes God's ways are hard to understand;
We want to ask "Why," to follow His hand.
Sometimes when tragedy comes from above,
It tempts us to waver, to doubt His love.

But God is infinitely wise and good,
He is too lofty to be understood.
His love is endless; His kindness is great.
He is too wise to leave one thing to fate.

Though His purpose may be unknown to us,
We cling to the Rock; in Him we must trust.
To Him we can run; with Him we can plead,
An ever-present help in time of need.

Our hearts they ache, our minds they probe,
But ultimately we must learn from Job.
The Lord who gives can also take away,
His name must be blessed each and every day.

We may wonder why He would make us weep;
His ways unsearchable, His knowledge deep.
So freely cry, tears and grief are His gifts,
By His grace He heals, by His strength He lifts.

(Based on Rom. 11:33; Ps. 46:1; 18:2; Job 1:21)[1]

Whate'er my God ordains is right

By Samuel Rodigast

Whate'er my God ordains is right:
His holy will abideth;
I will be still whate'er he doth;
And follow where he guideth;
He is my God; though dark my road,
He holds me that I shall not fall:
Wherefore to him I leave it all.

Whate'er my God ordains is right:
He is my Friend and Father;
He suffers naught to do me harm,
Though many storms may gather;
Now I may know both joy and woe,
Some day I shall see clearly
That he hath loved me dearly.

Whate'er my God ordains is right:
Though now this cup, in drinking,
May bitter seem to my faint heart,
I take it, all unshrinking.
My God is true; each morn anew
Sweet comfort yet shall fill my heart,
And pain and sorrow shall depart.[2]

Jesus, lover of my soul

By Charles Wesley

Jesus, lover of my soul, let me to Thy bosom fly,
While the nearer waters roll, while the tempest still is high:
Hide me, O my Saviour, hide, till the storm of life is past;
Safe into the haven guide, O receive my soul at last!

Other refuge have I none, hangs my helpless soul on Thee;
Leave, ah! leave me not alone, still support and comfort me!
All my trust on Thee is stayed, all my help from Thee I bring;
Cover my defenceless head with the shadow of Thy wing.

Thou, O Christ, art all I want; more than all in Thee I find:
Raise the fallen, cheer the faint, heal
the sick, and lead the blind.
Just and holy is thy name; I am all unrighteousness;
False and full of sin I am, Thou art full of truth and grace.

Plenteous grace with Thee is found, grace to cover all my sin;
Let the healing streams abound; make
and keep me pure within:
Thou of life the fountain art, freely let me take of Thee;
Spring Thou up within my heart, rise to all eternity.[3]

Children of the heav'nly Father

By Karolina W. Sandell-Berg

Children of the heav'nly Father
Safely in His bosom gather;
Nestling bird nor star in Heaven
Such a refuge e'er was given.

God His own doth tend and nourish;
In His holy courts they flourish;
From all evil things He spares them;
In His mighty arms He bears them.

Neither life nor death shall ever
From the Lord His children sever;
Unto them His grace He showeth,
And their sorrows all He knoweth.

Though He giveth or He taketh,
God His children ne'er forsaketh;
His the loving purpose solely
To preserve them pure and holy.

Lo, their very hairs He numbers,
And no daily care encumbers
Them that share His ev'ry blessing
And His help in woes distressing.

Praise the Lord in joyful numbers:
Your Protector never slumbers.
At the will of your Defender
Ev'ry foeman must surrender.[4]

Come, ye disconsolate[5]

By Thomas Moore and Thomas Hastings

Come, ye disconsolate, where'er ye languish,
Come to the Mercy-seat, fervently kneel.
Here bring your wounded hearts, here tell your anguish;
Earth has no sorrow that Heaven cannot heal.

Joy of the desolate, Light of the straying,
Hope of the penitent, fadeless and pure;
Here speaks the Comforter, tenderly saying,
Earth has no sorrow that Heaven cannot cure.

Here see the Bread of Life; see waters flowing
Forth from the throne of God, pure from above.
Come to the feast of love; come, ever knowing
Earth has no sorrow but Heaven can remove.[6]

123

Heaven desired

Author unknown

O my Lord,
May I arrive where means of grace cease
    and I need no more to fast, pray,
      weep, watch,
      be tempted, attend preaching and sacrament;
where nothing defiles,
where is no grief, sorrow, sin, death,
            separation, tears, pale face, languid body,
            aching joints, feeble infancy, decrepit age,
            peccant humours, pining sickness,
            griping fears, consuming cares;
where is personal completeness;
where the more perfect the sight
    the more beautiful the object,
the more perfect the appetite
    the sweeter the food,
the more musical the ear
    the more pleasant the melody,
the more complete the soul
    the more happy its joys,
where is full knowledge of thee.
Here I am an ant, and as I view a nest of ants
    so dost thou view me and my fellow-creatures;
But as an ant knows not me, my nature, my thoughts,
    so here I cannot know thee clearly.

But there I shall be near thee,
 dwell with my family,
 stand in thy presence chamber,
 be an heir of thy kingdom,
   as the spouse of Christ,
   as a member of his body,
   one with him who is with thee,
 and exercise all my powers of body and soul
   in the enjoyment of thee.
As praise in the mouth of thy saints is comely,
 so teach me to exercise this divine gift,
 when I pray, read, hear, see, do,
 in the presence of people and of my enemies,
 as I hope to praise thee eternally hereafter.[7]

Under His wings

By William O. Cushing

Under His wings I am safely abiding;
Tho' the night deepens and tempests are wild,
Still I can trust Him; I know He will keep me;
He has redeemed me, and I am His child.

Under His wings, under His wings,
Who from His love can sever?
Under His wings my soul shall abide,
Safely abide forever.

Under His wings, what a refuge in sorrow!
How the heart yearningly turns to His rest!
Often when earth has no balm for my healing,
There I find comfort, and there I am blest.

Under His wings, O what precious enjoyment!
There will I hide till life's trials are o'er;
Sheltered, protected, no evil can harm me;
Resting in Jesus I'm safe evermore.[8]

Consolation

By Georgie Tillman Snead

How sweet amid earth's wild alarms,
To feel the everlasting arms;
To know He careth day by day,
And will not turn our pray'r away.

He hears our plea, He sends relief,
He gives us solace from our grief;
He sends refreshing showers down,
And thus our lives with blessings crown.

We'll 'bide in Him, then ev'ry hour,
And we will feel His sov'reign pow'r;
He'll be our strength, our refuge sweet,
And all our faith He will complete.

Oh, let our pray'rs like incense rise
Unto the Lord of earth and skies;
Give thanks for all His mercy shown,
Praise Him who claims us for His own.[9]

Sovereign Ruler of the skies

By John Ryland

Sovereign Ruler of the skies!
Ever gracious, ever wise!
All my times are in Thy hand,
All events at thy command.

He that formed me in the womb,
He shall guide me to the tomb.
All my times shall ever be
Ordered by his wise decree.

Times of sickness, times of health;
Times of poverty or wealth;
Times of trial and times of grief;
Times of triumph and relief;

Times the tempter's power to prove;
Times to taste a saviour's love.
All must come, and last, and end,
As shall please my Heavenly Friend.

Plagues and deaths around me fly.
Till he bids I cannot die.
Not a single dart can hit,
Till the God of love thinks fit.

O Thou gracious, wise, and just,
In Thy hands my life I trust.
Thee, at all times, will I bless.
Having Thee, I all possess.[10]

The way of the cross leads home

By Jesse B. Pounds

I must needs go home by the way of the cross,
There's no other way but this;
I shall ne'er get sight of the Gates of Light,
If the way of the cross I miss.

The way of the cross leads home,
The way of the cross leads home;
It is sweet to know, as I onward go,
The way of the cross leads home.

I must needs go on in the blood-sprinkled way,
The path that the Savior trod,
If I ever climb to the heights sublime,
Where the soul is at home with God.

Then I bid farewell to the way of the world,
To walk in it nevermore;
For my Lord says, "Come," and I seek my home,
Where He waits at the open door.[11]

O refuge near

By Jonathan Allston

O refuge near, our strength in weakness,
forever in His hands secure;
Emmanuel, God always with us,
Almighty One within my soul.
I'll never fear the roaring waters; the
tempests know the One in me.
The hands that hold the stars in motion
are holding me in love and care.

Consider well His lovingkindness; He
never will your soul forsake.
Find rest in Him; yet in your resting, spend
all your strength for Jesus' sake.
Look on His face, so bruised and bleeding;
look on His soul that knew no sin.
The God of love was pleased to wound Him
when our soul's sins were laid on Him.

Are you too strong to rest in His strength,
or is your mind too wise for Him?
Do riches bring more love and mercy than
Jesus Christ the perfect Lamb?
Does He who made you lack in power
or He who died too short on love?
Can you think on those nails run through His
hands and claim He's not enough for you?

My dearest Lord, Your love o'erwhelms me;
my cup can't hold the gifts You give.
The pages of my life are empty
for you to fill just as You wish.
I want for You to write my story;
blot out the words that I have penned.
Fill every page for Your own glory and end
it with the words, "Well done!"[12]

Lord, You are my everything

By Jackie Arnoldi

Lord, You are my Comfort.
When hard times come my way,
Your presence never leaves me.
You are with me all the way.

Lord, You are my Strength.
When I grow weary in this land,
Never will I falter.
I'm upheld by Your right hand.

Lord, You are my Peace.
You are the calmer of my fears.
When worries overwhelm me,
Your love wipes away my tears.

Lord, You're my Sustainer,
You hold me safely at Your side.
I will make it through the storms,
Because in You I will abide.

Lord, You are my Joy.
Amidst the trials and the pain,
I trust Your sovereign care.
I see the Son between the rain.

Lord, You are my Rock,
My firm foundation, solid ground.
You are mighty and unchanging,
You have no limits and no bounds.

Lord, You are my Everything,
Life with You is so complete.
One day You'll bring me home to You,
And I will worship at Your feet.

Dedicated to my mom, whose Lord was her Everything
Jean Pitz
June 9, 1953—April 12, 2008[13]

133

Sample memorial services

As a general rule, memorial services should be on the brief side. The bereaved are exhausted from the numerous decisions of previous days, and sometimes months or even years in the case of prolonged sickness. Therefore, their attention spans will not be long. However, the minister who is responsible for officiating must also be certain that the service is substantial enough to properly honor the deceased and recognize the value of the life that has been lived. Sherwin Nuland writes, "The greatest dignity to be found in death is the dignity of the life that preceded it."[1] Since this is basically true, but more importantly because of the sanctity of human life, memorial services must always be handled with utmost dignity and respect. The following are some sample orders of service for the funerals of both unbelievers and believers.

When the deceased is probably an unbeliever

Sample 1

Prelude

Welcome: Thank you for being here today to share in this special service in honor of _____. We have come to express our final goodbyes to a wife, mother, grandmother, relative, and friend who has impacted all of our lives in some way.

Obituary

Scripture: Psalm 27

Prayer

Special memories from family

Song: The Lord's Prayer (Matt. 6:9–13; music by Albert Hay Mallotte; arr. Donald Hustad, 1953)

Scripture: Psalm 90

Message: Why Are We Here? [see Chapter 6]

Prayer

Song: How Great Thou Art (Carl Gustav Boberg; tr. Stuart K. Hine)

(Funeral director to close the service with instructions.)

SAMPLE 2

[This service is designed for an army veteran, and is particularly appropriate in the US. The principles upon which the service is based could be applied more generally to recognize the achievements of people in other fields of service.]

Prelude

Welcome: Thank you for being here today to share in this special service in memory of one of our veterans, _____. Let's take a few moments to reflect on John's life.

Obituary

Scripture: Psalm 46

Prayer

Song: a patriotic hymn

Message: Bringing Life Out of Death [see Chapter 5]

Prayer

Song: America, the Beautiful (Katharine Lee Bates)

(Funeral director to close the service with thank you and announcements.)

When the deceased is a believer

SAMPLE 1

Song: Amazing Grace (John Newton)

Welcome: Thank you for being here today to share in this special service in honor of _____. As we reflect on the part that _____ played in each of our lives, let us remember some of the highlights of his/her life.

Obituary: based on the outline given in Ecclesiastes 3:1–8

Scripture: Psalm 46

Prayer

Song: O the Deep, Deep Love of Jesus (Samuel Trevor Francis)

Message: Lessons From the Death of Lazarus [based on John 11, not included in this book]

Prayer

Scripture: 1 Thessalonians 4:13–18

Song: How Great Thou Art (Carl Gustav Boberg; tr. Stuart K. Hine)

(Funeral director to close the service with thank you and announcements.)

Sample 2

This memorial service was in honor of Jean Pitz, who fought a courageous battle against cancer prior to receiving the eternal reward of her faith. It is unusually long due to the breadth of her influence and the desire of her family, as well as her church, to truly celebrate her going home to the Lord.

Song: God Makes No Mistakes (Mac and Beth Lynch)

Welcome

Obituary: based on the outline given in Ecclesiastes 3:1–8

Scripture: John 11:1–36

Prayer

Congregational hymn: Rejoice in the Lord (Ron Hamilton)

Congregational hymn: When We See Christ (Esther Kerr Rusthoi)

Special memories from family

Message: The Reality of Death and Eternal Life [see Chapter 7]

Ministry of music: It Is Not Death to Die (H. A. Cesar; tr. George W. Bethune)

Scripture: 1 John 5:11–13

Congregational hymn: In Christ Alone (Keith Getty and Stuart Townend)

Closing prayer.

FOR FURTHER HELP AND INFORMATION

Resources to strengthen pastoral ministry and counseling

Baxter, Richard, *The Reformed Pastor* (1656; 1974, Edinburgh: Banner of Truth).

Bridges, Charles, *The Christian Ministry* (1830; 1967, Edinburgh: Banner of Truth).

Bridges, Jerry, *Trusting God* (Colorado Springs, CO: NavPress, 1988).

Dever, Mark, *Nine Marks of a Healthy Church* (Wheaton, IL: Crossway, 2004).

Duncan, J. Ligon, and Hunt, Susan, *Women's Ministry in the Local Church* (Wheaton, IL: Crossway, 2006).

Elliff, Tom, *A Passion for Prayer* (Wheaton, IL: Crossway, 1998).

Kuiper, R. B., *God-Centred Evangelism* (London: Banner of Truth, 1966).

MacArthur, John, and the Master's Seminary Faculty, *Rediscovering Pastoral Ministry* (Dallas: Word, 1995).

Nettles, Thomas J., *By His Grace and For His Glory* (Lake Charles, LA: Cor Meum Tibi, 2002).

Piper, John, *Brothers, We are Not Professionals* (Nashville, TN: B & H, 2002).

Powlison, David, *Seeing with New Eyes* (Phillipsburg, NJ: P & R, 2003).

——*Speaking Truth In Love: Counsel in Community* (Winston-Salem, NC: Punch Press, 2005).

——(ed.), *The Journal of Biblical Counseling on CD-ROM, Version 2.0.* (Glenside, PA: Christian Counseling & Educational Foundation, 1977–2005).

Shaw, John, *The Character of a Pastor According to God's Heart* (Ligonier, PA: Soli Deo Gloria, 1992).

Spurgeon, Charles H., *An All-Round Ministry* (Pasadena, TX: Pilgrim, 1983).

Tautges, Paul, *Delight in the Word* (Enumclaw, WA: Pleasant Word, 2007).

Thomas, Curtis C., *Life in the Body of Christ* (Cape Coral, FL: Founders Press, 2006).

Watson, Thomas, *A Body of Divinity* (1692; 1965, London: Banner of Truth).

Resources on grief, comfort, and the sovereignty of God in suffering

Baxter, Richard, *Dying Thoughts* (1683; 2004, Edinburgh: Banner of Truth).

Bruce, James W. III., *From Grief to Glory: A Book of Comfort for Grieving Parents* (Edinburgh: Banner of Truth, 2008). Also, see his website: www.grieftoglory.com.

Edwards, Jonathan, *Heaven: A World of Love* (Pocket Puritans; Edinburgh: Banner of Truth, 2008).

Howard, Deborah, *Sunsets: Reflections for Life's Final Journey* (Wheaton, IL: Crossway, 2005).

Kaiser, Walter C., *Grief and Pain* (Fearn: Christian Focus, 2004).

Ketcham, R. T., *Christ: The Comforter in Sorrow* (Schaumburg, IL: Regular Baptist Press, n.d.).

Piper, John, and Taylor, Justin, (eds.), *Suffering and the Sovereignty of God* (Wheaton, IL: Crossway, 2006).

Tripp, Paul David, *Grief: Finding Hope Again* (Greensboro, NC: New Growth Press, 2004).

Poetry, prayers, and hymn stories

Bennett, Arthur, (ed.), *The Valley of Vision* (Edinburgh: Banner of Truth, 1975).

MacArthur, John, Tada, Joni Eareckson, and Wolgemuth, Robert and Bobbie, *O Worship the King: Hymns of Assurance and Praise to Encourage Your Heart* (Wheaton, IL: Crossway, 2000).

——*When Morning Gilds the Skies: Hymns of Heaven and Our Eternal Hope* (Wheaton, IL: Crossway, 2002).

Morgan, Robert J., *Then Sings My Soul: 150 of the World's Greatest Hymn Stories* (Nashville, TN: Thomas Nelson, 2003).

Moments with the Book: www.mwtb.org.

Osbeck, Kenneth, *101 Hymn Stories* (Grand Rapids, MI: Kregel, 1982).

——*101 More Hymn Stories* (Grand Rapids, MI: Kregel, 1985).

Standfield, Anne, *Seasons of Comfort and Joy* (Leominster: Day One, 2008).

Websites with biblical counseling resources

Biblical Counseling Center: www.biblicalcounselingcenter.org

Christian Counsel & Educational Foundation: www.ccef.org

Counsel One Another: www.counseloneanother.blogspot.com

Delight in the Word Ministries: www.delightintheword.org

Faith Biblical Counseling: www.faithlafayette.org

Grief to Glory: www.grieftoglory.com

Institute for Biblical Counseling and Discipleship: www.ibcd.org

Institute for Nouthetic Studies: www.nouthetic.org

International Association of Biblical Counselors: www.iabc.net

National Association of Nouthetic Counselors: www.nanc.org

Return to the Word: www.returntotheword.org

Strengthening Ministries: www.mackministries.org

Women Helping Women: www.elysefitzpatrick.com

ENDNOTES

Preface

1 Paul David Tripp, *Grief: Finding Hope Again* (Greensboro, NC: New Growth Press, 2004), p. 8.

Introduction

1 Cevilla D. Martin, "His Eye Is on the Sparrow" (1905).

2 Warren W. Wiersbe, *Be Comforted* (Wheaton, IL: Scripture Press, 1992), p. 7.

3 Joni Eareckson Tada and Steve Estes, *When God Weeps* (Grand Rapids, MI: Zondervan, 1997), p. 202.

Part 1

1 Deborah Howard, *Sunsets: Reflections for Life's Final Journey* (Wheaton, IL: Crossway, 2005), p. 35. All italics within non-scriptural quotations are the original writer's. Italicized words or phrases within Scripture quotations, unless stated otherwise, indicate emphasis added by this author.

2 Walter C. Kaiser, *Grief and Pain* (Fearn: Christian Focus, 2004), p. 113.

Chapter 1

1 Jonathan Allston, "O Refuge Near" (verse 1 of an unpublished hymn, used by permission).

2 *How Firm a Foundation*, "K" in Rippon's *Selection of Hymns* (1787).

3 Dustin Shramek, "Waiting for the Morning During the Long Night of Weeping," in John Piper and Justin Taylor, (eds.), *Suffering and the Sovereignty of God* (Wheaton, IL: Crossway, 2006), p. 177.

4 James W. Bruce, III, *From Grief to Glory: A Book of Comfort for Grieving Parents* (Edinburgh: Banner of Truth, 2008), pp. 70–71.

5 George A. Young, *God Leads His Dear Children Along* (1903).

6 Kaiser, *Grief and Pain*, p. 43.

7 Michael Green, *Illustrations for Biblical Preaching* (Grand Rapids, MI: Baker, 1982), p. 406.

8 Author unknown. Every pastor should keep a supply of this tract-size poem on hand to place inside sympathy cards or to use on personal visits. I have used it for over a decade and it has brought much encouragement to sufferers. It is published by a literature ministry called Moments with the Book. Check out their great selection of comforting poems at www.mwtb.org.

Chapter 2

1 Richard Baxter, *Dying Thoughts* (1683; 2004, Edinburgh: Banner of Truth), p. 88.

2 See Appendix 4.

3 Tel Asiado, http://christianmusic. suite101.com/article.cfm/be_still_ my_soul_k_von_schlegel; accessed August 25, 2008.

4 Katharina von Schlegel; tr. Jane L. Borthwick, "Be Still, My Soul" (1752).

Chapter 3

1 H. A. Cesar Malan, "It Is Not Death to Die" (c. 1832; tr. George W. Bethune, 1805–1862; www.lutheran-hymnal. com, accessed July 15, 2008). A newer version, recently released by

Sovereign Grace Ministries (www.sovereigngraceministries.org), was sung at Jean Pitz's memorial service.

2 Tripp, *Grief*, p. 4.

3 C. H. Spurgeon, "The Hope Laid Up in Heaven," in Warren W. Wiersbe, (ed.), *Classic Sermons on Hope* (Grand Rapids, MI: Kregel, 1994), p. 125.

Chapter 4

1 George Schultz in Kiron K. Skinner, Annelise Anderson, and Martin Anderson, (eds.), *Reagan: A Life in Letters* (New York: Free Press, 2003), p. x.

2 Ibid., p. ix.

Chapter 6

1 George Bennard, "The Old Rugged Cross" (1913).

2 Cited in Haddon Robinson, *Biblical Preaching*, (Grand Rapids, MI: Baker, 1980), pp. 168–169.

Chapter 7

1 This message from Jean Pitz's memorial service is included here by permission of her husband, Jerome Pitz.

2 Keith Getty and Stuart Townend, "In Christ Alone" (2001).

Chapter 8

1 This message from Seth's memorial service is included here by permission of his parents, William and Carolyn Freel.

2 Bruce, *From Grief to Glory*, p. 29. In the providence of God, I stumbled upon this book one week prior to my first publication deadline for this book. I highly recommend you purchase copies as gifts for parents

who have lost children. If you do not know anyone in this situation now, buy a few copies anyway to keep on hand for when you do meet such people. The death of children is more common than we realize.

3 Ron Hamilton, "Rejoice in the Lord" (1978).

Part 3

1 Shramek, "Waiting for the Morning," p. 177.

2 Howard, *Sunsets*, p. 43.

Chapter 9

1 Bryan Jeffrey Leech, "We Are God's People" (1976).

2 Quoted by Kevin Ruffcorn in James D. Berkley, (ed.), *Leadership Handbook of Outreach and Care* (Grand Rapids, MI: Baker, 1994), p. 226.

3 Ibid., p. 226

4 Tripp, *Grief*, p. 11.

5 Paul Tautges, *Counsel Your Flock* (Leominster: Day One, 2009).

Chapter 10

1 In keeping with the apostolic teaching found in 1 Timothy 2:11–15, women are not to function in the capacity of a pastor-elder or deacon. These leadership roles are reserved for men in the church (1 Tim. 3:1–13; Titus 1:5–9). However, women should definitely be involved in ministries of compassion for the sick, dying, and bereaved. Also, men who are not necessarily official leaders in the church need to be trained to make these important visits as well. The

Bible teaches that all believers are "ministers" to one degree or another.

Appendix 2

1 From Paul Tautges, *Delight in the Word* (Enumclaw, WA: Pleasant Word, 2007), pp. 80–81.

2 Cited by Derek W. H. Thomas, *What Is Providence?* (Phillipsburg, NJ: P & R, 2008), pp. 35–36.

3 Charles Wesley, "Jesus, Lover of My Soul" (1740).

4 Karolina W. Sandell-Berg, "Children of the Heavenly Father" (1858; tr. from Swedish to English by Ernst W. Olson in 1925).

5 The word "disconsolate" means sad beyond comforting.

6 Stanzas 1–2 by Thomas Moore (1779–1852) and stanza 3 by Thomas Hastings (1784–1872); in *The Handbook to the Lutheran Hymnal* (St. Louis, MO: Concordia, 1942), p. 374.

7 In Arthur Bennett, (ed.), *The Valley of Vision* (Edinburgh: Banner of Truth, 1975), pp. 372–373.

8 William O. Cushing, "Under His Wings" (1924).

9 Georgie Tillman Snead, "Consolation" (1929).

10 John Ryland, "Sovereign Ruler of the Skies" (1753–1825)

11 Jesse B. Pounds, "The Way of the Cross Leads Home" (1906).

12 Jonathan Allston, "O Refuge Near" (previously unpublished hymn, used by permission).

13 Jackie Arnoldi, "Lord, You Are My Everything" (previously unpublished poem, used by permission).

Appendix 3

1 Sherwin Nuland, *How We Die* (New York: Vintage Books, 1993), p. 241.

Ministering the Master's way series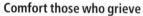